CRASH COURSE

— IN —

BEATING

TEXAS

HOLD'EM

CRASH COURSE

—— IN ——

BEATING TEXAS HOLD'EM

AVERY CARDOZA

CARDOZA
PUBLISHING

To Sara Gaz

Cardoza Publishing is the foremost gaming publisher in the world, with a library of over 175 up-to-date and easy-to-read books and strategies. These authoritative works are written by the top experts in their fields and with more than 8,500,000 books in print, represent the best-selling and most popular gaming books anywhere.

FIRST EDITION

Copyright © 2006 by Avery Cardoza
- All Rights Reserved -

Library of Congress Catalog Card No: 2005920568
ISBN: 1-58042-165-2

Visit our web site—www.cardozapub.com—or write for a full list of books and computer strategies.

CARDOZA PUBLISHING
P.O. Box 1500, Cooper Station, New York, NY 10276
Phone (800) 577-WINS
email: cardozapub@aol.com
www.cardozapub.com

TABLE OF CONTENTS

1. INTRODUCTION

"I'm all-in!" Those are the classic words of action in no-limit hold'em that make the game so riveting, so exciting, such a great spectator sport on television. When a player puts it all on the line with one bet, the drama, simply put, is thrilling. You too can be part of this excitement—the money, the fame, and of course, the fun!

This book covers every aspect of Texas hold'em, from the basics of play and hand values to the various bets possible. You'll learn how to beat limit and no-limit cash games and tournaments and how to think and play from every position at the table and with every type of hand. We'll also go over specific strategies for the preflop, flop, turn, and river.

Texas hold'em, as you'll see, is quite simple to play, but to master the game, well, there's a lot to learn. However, the learning curve is less steep if you understand and play by some basic principles. The good news is that you don't need to memorize much or even be mathematically inclined because hold'em, particularly the no-limit variety, is about reading people—and you've been doing that your whole life. Apply that basic skill to poker situations and you'll be okay. And if you follow the advice in this book, with a little luck, you might be *very* okay.

Okay, we have a lot to cover. There's a big tournament coming up soon, and you might just be at that final table, and hopefully, playing against me!

2. OVERVIEW

Texas hold'em, or **hold'em**, as the game is more commonly known, is played as high poker, that is, the player with the best and highest five card combination at the showdown will have the winning hand and collect the money in the pot. The pot can also be won by a player when all of his opponents fold their hands at any point before the showdown, leaving one player alone to claim the pot—even though he may not actually have held the best hand!

Your final five-card hand in hold'em will be made up of the best five-card combination of the seven total cards available to you. These include the **board**, five cards dealt face-up in the middle of the table, cards which are shared by all players, and your **pocket cards** or **hole cards**, two cards dealt face-down that can be used by you alone. For example, your final hand could be composed of your two pocket cards and three cards from the board, one pocket card and four from the board, or simply all five board cards.

At the beginning of a hand, each player is dealt two face-down cards. Then each player gets a chance to exercise his betting options. Next, three cards are dealt simultaneously on the table for all players to share. This is called the **flop**, and it is followed by another round of betting. A fourth board card, called the **turn**, is then dealt, and it too is followed by a round of betting. One final community card is dealt in the center of the table, making five total. This is the **river**. If two or more players remain in the hand, it is followed by the fourth and final betting round.

When all bets have concluded, there is the **showdown**, in which the highest ranking hand in play wins the **pot**—the accumulation of bets that are kept in the center of the table. The pot can also be won by a player when all of his opponents fold their hands at any point before the showdown, leaving one player alone to claim the pot—even though he may not actually have held the best hand!

FLOP	TURN	RIVER

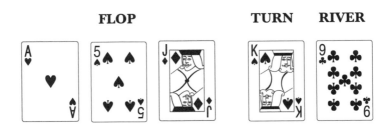

3. TYPES OF HOLD'EM GAMES

Poker can be played in two basic ways—as a cash game or in a tournament format. While tournaments get all the television coverage, the more popular games being played in cardrooms are actually the cash games. There are also various betting structures commonly played, and this section will go over the basic ones you'll find in both cash games and tournaments.

◆ CASH GAMES ◆

In a **cash game**, the chips you play with represent real money. If you go broke, you can always dig in to your pocket for more money. If you give the poker room $200 in cash, you get $200 worth of chips in return. If you build it up to $375, you can quit and convert your chips to cash anytime you want.

Your goal in a cash game is to win as much money as you can, or if things are going poorly, at least to lose as little as possible.

◆ TOURNAMENTS ◆

In a **tournament**, every player starts with an equal number of chips and plays until one player holds them all. Your goal in a tournament is to survive as long as you can. At the very least, you want to survive long enough to earn prizes, usually money, and in the best case scenario, to win it all, become the champion, and win the biggest prize.

As players lose their chips, they are eliminated from the tournament. Unlike a cash game, where the chips are the equivalent of cash money, **tournament chips** are only valuable in the tournament itself and have no cash value.

♦ BETTING STRUCTURES ♦

Poker has three different types of betting structures: limit, pot-limit, and no-limit. These structures don't change the basic way the games are played, only the amount of money that can be bet. The big difference between the three structures is the strategy. The amount you can bet changes the hands that you should play, when you should play them, and how much you should risk in any given situation.

In cardrooms, the betting limits of casino games are generally posted at the table or you will be directed to the game of your choice by the personnel in the poker room. In private games, the betting limits are prearranged and agreed upon by the players in advance or on the spot, but always before the cards are dealt.

Let's take a brief look at each betting structure.

♠ Limit Poker

In **limit poker**, the most common game played in cardrooms and casinos for cash, all bets are divided into a two-tier structure, such as $1/$2, $3/$6, $5/$10, $10/$20, and $15/$30, with the larger limit bets being exactly double the lower limit. On the preflop and flop, all bets and raises must be at the lower limit, and on the turn and river, all bets double and are made at the higher limit. Unless a player is short-stacked and cannot meet the required amount, all bets must be at the preestablished limits of the game. For example, in a $5/$10 limit game, when the lower limit of betting is in effect, all bets and raises must be in $5 increments. When the upper range is in effect, all bets and raises must be in $10 increments.

Unless a player is short-stacked and cannot meet the required amount, all bets must be at the preestablished limits of the game.

One form of limit poker, called **spread-limit**, allows you to bet any amount between the minimum and maximum amounts specified for the game. Spread limit is typically played in very low stakes games. For example, in a $1-$5 game, you may bet or raise $1, $2, $3, $4, or $5 before the flop, or on the flop, turn, or river. There is also a $1-$4-$8 spread-limit format where all bets on the preflop and flop can be anywhere from $1 to $4, and on the turn, and river, from $1 to $8.

♠ No-Limit Poker

No-limit hold'em is the exciting no-holds barred style of poker played in the World Series of Poker main event and seen on television by millions weekly on the World Poker Tour and stations such as The Travel Channel and ESPN. No-limit is usually associated with Texas hold'em, but this style of betting can be played in any variation.

The prevailing feature of no-limit hold'em is that you can bet any amount up to what you have in front of you on the table *anytime* it is your turn. That exciting "all-in" call signals a player's intention to put all his chips on the line.

♠ Pot-Limit Poker

Pot-limit, the least popular of the three structures, is a blend between limit and no-limit. The minimum bet allowed in pot-limit is that of the big blind bet (which helps determine the size of the game), while the maximum bet allowed is defined by the size of the *pot*. For example, if $75 is currently in the pot, then $75 is the maximum bet allowed. The pot sizes in pot-limit quickly escalate to large amounts. Like no-limit, this betting structure is not for the timid.

4. THE HOLD'EM SETTING

♦ THE PLAYERS ♦

A typical cardroom hold'em game fields between eight to ten players. When nine players are seated, the game is called **nine-handed** and similarly with ten players, it is called, **ten-handed**. Hold'em can even be played with more players. For example, in the 2004 World Series of Poker, as a result of the fire marshall closing off one of the playing areas, players were redistributed to other tables and we played **eleven-handed** for a while. I have even heard of **twelve-handed** games. In fact, hold'em, can theoretically support as many as twenty-two players in a live game (and twenty-three online), though games with more than ten players are rarely played.

When a full compliment of players are at a table, the game is called a **ring game**. When there are fewer than eight players in a hold'em game, say six or seven, the game is called **short-handed**. That means that the table contains fewer than the normal amount of players. Short-handed games can have as few as three, four, or five total players as well. When there are just two players in a hold'em game—really, any poker game—it is called **head-to-head** of **heads-up** play.

But regardless of the number of players seated, the rules and procedures of the game are identical. The strategies, however, are greatly affected by the number of players you are competing against. The larger the number of players, the more powerful your average hand must be to make profitable bets. For example, playing the starting cards of A-6 in a ten-handed game would lose you a lot of money in the long run, but heads-up, against just one player, that A-6 would be powerful and profitable.

♦ THE DEALER ♦

In a casino or cardroom, the house will supply a dealer. He is not a participant in the betting or play of the game. His role is simply to shuffle the deck, deal the cards to the players, and direct the action so that the game runs smoothly. He will point out whose turn it is to play and pull bets into the pot after each round of cards. And at the showdown, he will announce the best hand, push the pot over to the winning player, then reshuffle the cards, and get ready for the next deal.

In a private game, one of the players is designated as the dealer. The dealer position changes with each hand, rotating around the table in a clockwise direction, with each player having a chance to deal. The dealer is still an active player in a private game and enjoys no advantage other than any positional edge he may have for the particular game played.

♦ SHUFFLING AND WASHING ♦

Starting with a fresh deck of cards, the dealer will turn the pack face up on the table and spread them out so all players can verify that the pack is complete with the full complement of 52 cards. The cards will be arranged by suit and in numerical order so it is easy for all the players and the dealer to see that the ace through the king of each of the four suits (hearts, diamonds, clubs, and spades) are all there.

The dealer will then turn over the cards so that only the

backs of the deck can be seen and spread them around the table as the first step in making the order of the cards random. This is called **washing** the deck. Sometimes the deck is washed with the cards face up as the first step, but either way, the point is to get a good, random mix of the cards. After the first hand is played out, the cards will no longer need to be verified by the players so the dealer will simply shuffle the cards for the next deal.

After washing, the dealer will then shuffle the deck in the traditional fashion. He will use a **cut card** (a separate colored plastic card made specifically for this purpose) to split the deck, and restack it with the bottom stack on top and the top stack on the bottom. Finally, before the cards are dealt, the dealer will make sure all mandatory bets (blinds and antes), if required, are in place. And then he will begin dealing.

♦ THE CARDROOM MANAGER OR TOURNAMENT DIRECTOR ♦

In a cardroom, the employee responsible for the supervision of poker games is the **cardroom manager**, or if there is a tournament in progress, the **tournament director**. When a dispute arises, the dealer or one of the players may call over the supervisor for a ruling. If a player gets out of hand and abusive, the supervisors may ask the player to act more appropriately and let that serve as a warning. If the situation warrants or the abuse or infractions of the rules or decorum of the game continues, the player may be given a "time out," and will be disallowed from play for say, ten or twenty minutes, twenty-four hours, or in extreme cases, permanently.

♦ THE POKER TABLE ♦

In a cardroom, the players and dealer sit around a table built to accommodate the game of poker, and often, specifically one built for the game of hold'em. (Hold'em tables are larger than seven-card stud tables). The typical cardroom hold'em table is oblong and can hold up to ten players seated comfortably. At home, of course, any table can be used.

The dealer sits in the middle of the long side where there is an indentation cut into the table to facilitate access to the players. He will usually have a small rack in front of him where he can keep an extra deck of cards, chips, cash, and a few other items. In a cash game, he may also have a drop box where he will deposit money taken out of the pot as the house commission (see "Rake," later).

♦ CHIPS AND MONEY ♦

Poker is almost always played with **chips**, thin, circular clay or plastic units that are assigned specific values, such as $1, $5, $25, and $100. Poker can also be played for cash, but this is discouraged in cardrooms as it slows down the game. Chips are much more practical to use.

In casino poker, the standard denominations of chips are $1, $5, $25, $100, and sometimes $10 units as well. In big money games, you can find $1,000, $5,000, and if the game is big enough, $25,000 and $100,000 chips! While some casinos use their own color code, the standard color scheme of poker chips is: $1-blue or white, $5-red, $25-green, and $100-black.

To receive chips in a cardroom, give the dealer cash, and he'll give you back the equivalent value in chips. This exchange of cash for chips is called a **buy-in** and is usually done right at the table. Dealers will accept only cash for chips, so if you have traveler's checks, credit cards, or other forms of money, you need to exchange these for cash at the area marked **Casino Cashier**. Then, with cash in hand, you can return to the poker table and buy chips.

In private games, players generally use chips, though

sometimes the game will be cash only. When chips are used, one player acts as the **bank** or **banker**. He converts players' cash buy-ins to equivalent values in chips. The most common denominations of chips used in private games are one unit, five units, ten units, twenty-five units, and one-hundred units. A unit can equal 1¢, $1, or whatever value is agreed upon by the players. Now, with the recent interest in poker, many home games are using casino style chips for their games.

♦ THE DECK OF CARDS ♦

Hold'em is played with a standard pack of fifty-two cards consisting of thirteen ranks, ace through king in each of four suits (hearts, clubs, diamonds, spades). The ace is the best and highest card, followed in descending order by the king, queen, jack, 10, 9, 8, 7, 6, 5, 4, 3, and then the **deuce** or 2, which is the lowest ranked card. The king, queen, and jack are known as **picture cards** or **face cards**.

When the cards are held together in various combinations, they form hands of different strengths. These are called **hand rankings** or **poker rankings**.

THE FOUR SUITS

hearts   clubs   diamonds   spades

The four suits in poker have no basic value in the determination of winning hands. As you shall see, it is not the value of the individual cards that reigns supreme in poker, but the *combination of cards* which determine the value of a player's hand.

♦ CARD ABBREVIATIONS ♦

Cards are referred to in writing by the following commonly used symbols: ace (A), king (K), queen (Q), jack (J), and all others directly by their numerical value, 10, 9, 8, 7, 6, 5, 4, 3, and 2.

5. POKER FUNDAMENTALS

Hold'em is played as high poker, that is, the player with the highest five-card combination at the showdown will have the winning hand and collect the money in the pot. Of course, if all players but one are out of the pot before the showdown, the remaining player will win regardless of what hand he holds.

♦ OBJECT OF THE GAME ♦

Your goal is to win as many chips as possible. In cash games, this means making as much money as you can, and in a tournament, this means being the last player left after all opponents have been knocked out, making you the biggest prize winner and the champion.

You can win only what your opponents risk, so pots will be of different sizes. They will vary from small ones, in which players have hands they are not willing to commit many chips to, to large ones where two or more players have strong hands they think will win and will push chips at each other in an effort to build the pot or induce opponents to throw away their cards and bow out of the hand.

Do not confuse the goal of winning chips with winning pots. It is not how many pots you win, but how much money. It is better to win one pot with $500 in chips than three pots with $100 each. In fact, the player who wins the most pots often is a player who ends up a loser! Why? He's playing too many hands, and while he's winning a lot of them, at the same time, he is losing a lot of other hands and for lots of chips since he is paying to see these hands through to the end. When those hands don't win, those losses add up quickly to big losses.

Poker is a game where every participant plays by himself and for himself alone against all other players. Collusion and partnership play are both illegal and considered cheating.

♦ HAND RANKINGS ♦

The standard poker rankings are used in hold'em. The royal flush is the highest, then the straight flush, four of a kind, full house, flush, straight, three of a kind, two pair, one pair, and then high card. The order in which cards are dealt or how they are displayed is irrelevant to the final value of the hand. For example, 7-7-K-A-5 is equivalent to A-K-7-7-5.

This is how the hands are formed:

♠ High-Card Hands

Hands that have no stronger combinations, such as a pair, two pair or better—simply five odd cards. 3-9-K-7-10, is a "king-high" hand. The highest ranking card in a high card hand, or if tied, the next highest untied card, will beat a lesser high card hand. A-K-J-10-4 beats A-K-J-3-2.

♠ One Pair

Two cards of equal rank. Example: 5-5-8-J-K. If two players are competing with one-pair hands, then the higher ranked of the pairs—aces highest, deuces lowest—wins the pot. And if two players have the same pair, then the highest side card would be used to determine the higher-ranking hand. 5-5-A-7-6 beats 5-5-K-Q-J, since the ace is a higher kicker than the king.

♠ Two Pair

Two pairs and an odd card. Example: 6-6-J-J-2. The highest pair of competing two-pair hands will win, or if the top pair is tied, then the second pair. If both pairs are equivalent, then the fifth card decides the winner. K-K-3-3-6 beats J-J-8-8-Q and K-K-2-2-A, but loses to K-K-3-3-9.

♠ Three of a Kind

Three cards of equal rank and two odd cards. Also called **trips** or a **set**. Example: Q-Q-Q-7-J. If two players hold a set, the higher ranked set will win, and if both players hold an equivalent set, then the highest odd card determines the winner. 7-7-7-4-2 beats 5-5-5-A-K, but loses to 7-7-7-9-5.

♠ Straight

Five cards of mixed suits in sequence, but it may not wrap around the ace. For example, Q-J-10-9-8 of mixed suits is a straight, but Q-K-A-2-3 is not—it's simply an ace-high hand. If two players hold straights, the higher straight card at the top end of the sequence will win. J-10-9-8-7 beats 5-4-3-2-A but would tie another player holding J-10-9-8-7.

♠ Flush

Five cards of the same suit. Example: K-10-9-5-3, all in diamonds. If two players hold flushes, the player with the highest card wins or if the highest card is tied, then the highest untied card. Suits have no relevance. Thus, Q-J-7-5-4 of diamonds beats Q-J-4-3-2 of spades.

♠ Full House

Three of a kind and a pair. Example: 5-5-5-9-9. If two players hold full houses, the player with the higher three of a kind wins. J-J-J-8-8 beats 7-7-7-A-A.

♠ Four of a Kind

Four cards of equal rank and an odd card. Also called **quads.** Example: K-K-K-K-3. If two players hold quads, the higher ranking quad will win the hand. K-K-K-K-3 beats 7-7-7-7-A and K-K-K-K-2.

♠ Straight Flush

Five cards in sequence, all in the same suit. Example: 7-6-5-4-3, all in spades. If two straight flushes are competing, the one with the highest card wins.

♠ Royal Flush

The A-K-Q-J-10 of the same suit, the best hand possible. No royal flush is higher than another.

♦ HOW TO READ YOUR HOLD'EM HAND ♦

You have all seven cards available to form your final five-card hand—any combination of your two hole cards and the five cards from the board. You can even use all five board cards. Let's look at an example.

YOU   **YOUR OPPONENT**

THE BOARD

Your best hand, three jacks, is made using your two pocket cards and one jack from the board. This beats your opponent's pair of aces, formed with one card from his hand and one from the board. In both instances, the other cards are not relevant. For example there is no need to say three jacks with an ace and a king versus two aces with a king, queen and jack—simply, three jacks versus two aces.

If the river card, the last card turned up on the board, had been a K♦ instead of a K♣, your opponent would have a diamond flush (formed with his two pocket diamonds and the three diamonds on the board), which would beat your set of jacks.

Let's say this was the situation:

YOU   **YOUR OPPONENT**

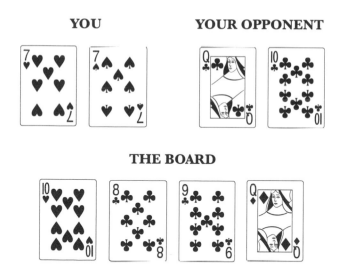

THE BOARD

In this hand, the turn card, the fourth on board, has given your opponent two pair, queens and tens. By itself, your pair of sevens is a big underdog, but you also have a straight draw— meaning that you have four cards to a straight. If either a jack or a 6 comes on the river, that will give you a straight. (Similarly, a **flush draw** is when you have four suited cards and need one more of that suit to make a flush.)

On the river, here is what comes:

THE BOARD

A jack! That is a great card for you, improving your hand to a straight. When your opponent turns over his cards, your heart jumps when you see that he has two pair because a straight is of higher rank and would make you a winner. But wait! By using all five board cards, he has formed a queen-high straight and as you look more carefully, you see that these five board cards give you a queen-high straight as well. So the hand is a push. You and your opponent would **chop** the pot, that is, you would split the pot evenly.

In this example, all five board cards were used to form both players' best hands. You would rather have seen a 6 than the jack because then you would have had the only straight and the winning hand. But if it had been the 6♣ or the river jack had been a club, your opponent would have made a flush (actually, a straight flush if it was a J♣!) and beaten your straight. So, as you can see, the very last card can turn a big underdog into a winner. You never know, or as Yogi Berra said, "It ain't over till it's over."

♦ BETTING OPTIONS ♦

When it is your turn to play, the following options, which apply to all forms of poker, are available to you:

1. Bet: Put chips at risk, that is, wager money, if no player has done so before you.

2. Call: Match a bet if one has been placed before your turn.

3. Raise: Increase the size of a current bet such that opponents, including the original bettor, must put additional money into the pot to stay active in a hand.

4. Fold: Give up your cards and opt out of play if a bet is due and you do not wish to match it. This forfeits your chance of competing for the pot.

5. Check: Stay active in a hand without making a bet and risking chips. This is only possible if no bets have been made.

The first three options—bet, call, and raise—are all a form of putting chips at risk in hopes of winning the pot. Once chips are bet and due, you must match that bet to continue playing for the pot or you must fold. Checking is not an option. If no chips are due, you can stay active in the hand without cost by checking.

If a bet has been made, each **active player**—one who has not folded—is faced with the same options: call, fold, or raise.

When a bet has been made, it no longer belongs to the bettor; it becomes the property of the pot, the communal collection of money that is up for grabs by all active players.

Betting continues in a round until the last bet or raise is called by all active players—or if all players have checked—at which point the betting round is over. A player may not raise his own bet when his betting turn comes around. He may raise only another player's bet or raise.

♦ THE SHOWDOWN ♦

If two or more players remain at the conclusion of all betting in the final betting round of a poker game, the showdown occurs. The **showdown** is the final act in a poker game where remaining players reveal their hands to determine the winner of the pot.

The player whose last bet or raise was called—or if all players checked, then the first to the left of the dealer position—turns over his cards first and reveals his hand. The player with the best hand at the showdown wins all the money in the pot. Players holding losing hands at the showdown may concede the pot without showing their cards.

In the event of a tie, the pot will be split evenly among the winners.

If only one player remains after the final betting round, or at any point during the game, there is no showdown. The remaining player automatically wins the pot and gets to collect all the chips.

♦ WHAT BETTING IS ALL ABOUT ♦

In poker, you compete for the pot, which is kept in the middle of the table. You'll make bets for one of three reasons:

1. You feel your hand has enough strength to win and you want to induce opponents to put more money into the pot.

2. You want to force opponents out of the pot so that the field is narrowed, since fewer players increases your chances of winning.

3. You want to induce all your opponents to fold so that you can win the pot uncontested.

♠ **PLAYING TIP** ♠

Never fold a hand, no matter how bad, when you can check and remain active for free.

♦ HOW TO BET ♦

A bet is made by either pushing the chips in front of you—an action which speaks for itself—or by verbally calling out the play, and *then* pushing the chips in front of you. Simply announce, "I call," "I bet," "I raise," or whatever clearly indicates your desire, and then push your chips out on the felt. Note that if you announce a check, bet, raise, or a fold, it is binding and you're committed to the action.

Your bet should be placed at least six inches toward the middle, but not so far that your chips mingle with those already in the pot and cannot be distinguished from them. That is, your chips should be far enough away from your own stack and the pot so that they are clearly seen not only as a bet, but as *your* bet.

Do not throw your chips into the actual pot, which is called **splashing the pot**. This protects all players from an opponent intentionally or unintentionally miscalling a bet. Betting properly also allows the amount of the wager to easily be verified while making it clear to all players that a bet or raise has been made.

To check, tap or knock on the table with your fingertips or hand or announce "I check" or "check." To fold, push your cards or toss them *face down* towards the dealer. It is illegal to show your cards to active players who are competing for the pot.

♠ **BE CAREFUL TO ANNOUNCE CALLS BEFORE EXPOSING CARDS!** ♠

In one game, I saw a player become so excited with his flush, that he turned up his cards on the river but didn't announce that he had called his opponent's bet. He also hadn't moved any chips to indicate a call. The dealer collected the flush, mucked the hand, and pushed the pot over to the other player. The player with the flush argued with the floorperson—but to no avail. According to the rules he had indeed mucked his cards since neither a verbal call nor a physical placement of a bet was made prior to his revealing his hand.

♦ POKER ETIQUETTE ♦

♠ Betting Etiquette

It is important to wait for your turn to play before announcing or revealing to any opponents what decision you will make. For example, if you know you're going to fold, you shouldn't toss your cards to the dealer before the action comes around to your position. And when you do give up your hand, pass the cards to the dealer face down, so that no other player can view them. If any cards are revealed to any one player, the rules of the game require that all players see them so that everyone is kept on equal footing.

It is improper and illegal to discuss your hand or another player's hand while a game is in progress. It is also very poor form to criticize other players strategy decisions, no matter how poor they appear to be. If you think an opponent plays poorly, then that's good news for you: go win his chips.

Another no-no is **string betting**. This is making a bet, and then adding to that bet with a second motion. For example, if you put $10 in front of your position as a bet, that is your final bet. You may not reach back and throw another $10 on top of that.

♠ Other Etiquette

Celebrating wins by shouting or taunting is considered very bad form at the poker table. Remember, your win is another player's loss. As good as you feel about the win, your opponent probably feels equally upset at the loss.

♦ THE ONE CHIP BET ♦

When there is a bet due your position, and you push a single chip out into the betting area—be it $5, $25, $100, or even $1,000—that chip is considered to be only a call unless you verbally state it's a raise *before* the chip is placed. For example, if a $10 bet is made and you toss a $100 chip into the pot without saying anything, your action will be considered a $10 call. Once that chip hits the felt, it is too late even if you announce "raise" afterwards; it will be taken to be a $10 call. If you say, "make it $100," or "raise," or some statement indicating this action before betting the chip, then the bet *will* be a raise.

If you're playing a no-limit game and are first to make a bet after the flop, a $100 chip will be taken to be a $100 bet. Unless you verbally call out a different amount, once the chip hits the felt, it is too late. It plays as it lays. It *is* a $100 bet. If you were playing a $10/$20 limit game, the bet will be only $10 on the flop, or $20 on the turn or river, as there can be no other bet possible. You will be given $80 or $90 change, as appropriate.

When you push two or more chips in front of you, this action is clear in no-limit. That amount in the pile is your bet or raise. In limit games, the amount will be either a call or a raise, depending on the amount placed.

♦ MINIMUM AND MAXIMUM BETS ♦

♠ Limit Poker

The minimum and maximum bets in limit games are strictly regulated according to the preset limits of the game. For example, $3/$6 and $5/$10 are two common limits.

The number of raises allowed in a round are also restricted, usually limited to three or four total according to the house rules for the cardroom. In other words, if there is a three-raise limit and the action goes bet, raise, reraise, and reraise, the raising would be **capped**. No more raises would be allowed for that round.

The exception to this rule comes into play when players are heads-up, in which case, there is no cap to the number of raises that can be made.

♠ No-Limit Poker

In no-limit cash games and tournaments, there is typically no cap to the number of raises allowed, though there are cardrooms that still impose the three- or four-raise rule. There is also no limit to how high a bet or raise can be. Players may raise as often as they like and for all their chips.

The minimum bet in no-limit must be at least the size of the big blind. Thus, if the big blind is $5, then the minimum allowed bet is $5. And raises must be at least equal to the size of the previous bet or raise in the round. For example, a $10 bet can be raised $30 more to make it $40 total. If a succeeding player reraises, he would have to make it at least $30 more—since that is the size of the last raise—for $70 total.

♦ TABLE STAKES, TAPPED OUT PLAYERS, AND SIDE POTS ♦

You may only bet or call bets up to the amount of money you have on the table. This is called **table stakes**. You are not allowed to withdraw money from your wallet, borrow from other players, or receive credit while a hand is in progress. Getting extra cash or chips is permissible only *before* the cards are dealt.

For example, in limit poker, if the bet is $25 and you only have $10, you may only call for $10. The remaining $15 and all future monies bet during this hand—except for bets by opponents to equal the $10—would be separated into a **side pot**. A player who has no more table funds from which to bet is **tapped-out**.

A tapped-out player can still receive cards until the showdown and play for the **main pot**, however, he can no longer bet in this hand and has no interest in the side pot. The other active players can continue to bet against each other for the money in the side pot in addition to remaining in competition for the main pot with the tapped-out player.

At the showdown, if the tapped-out player has the best hand, he receives only the money in the main pot. The side pot will be won by the player having the best hand among the remaining players. Should one of the other players hold the overall best hand, that player wins both the original pot and the side pot.

If only one opponent remains when a player taps out, then there is no more betting, and cards are played out until the showdown, where the best hand wins.

♦ THE RAKE ♦

Unlike other games offered in a casino setting, where players gamble against the house, poker is a game that pits players against one another, with each player trying to beat his fellow players out of money. Cardrooms act only as a host of poker games and make their money by taking a percentage of each pot, called a **rake**, as their fee for running the game. In low limit games and online, the rake can be anywhere from 5% to 10%, usually with a cap of $3 to $5 per pot. In higher limit games, the house typically charges players by time.

Time collection, where the house charges players by the half-hour or hour, is the preferred method of rakes. Generally speaking, this will come out to a smaller fee than the rakes taken out of the pot. While you generally don't have a choice given that you'll be playing where you'll be playing, you should be aware of the size rake that a cardroom collects, as it greatly impacts your profit potential. The rake, in a sense, serves as a tax. Obviously, the lower the rake, the better it is for your bottom line.

In tournaments, the house rake is collected up-front. For example, a tournament with a $500 entry fee may add $40 to the $500 so your real cost might be $540. The $500 goes into the prize pool for the players, while the $40 goes to the dealers as a tip and the house for its fee.

The rake is a very real cost of playing and will eat into your profits. For example, if you're playing dead-even poker against the other players, you will end up a loser because of the money you lose to the house through the rake. To show a profit in cardroom poker, you need to not only beat the other players, but earn enough profits to cover the cost of the rake. If a group of players play a rake game long enough, eventually, the house will have all the money!

So as you see, the amount of the rake removed from a game greatly affects your profit potential as a player. The lower the rake, the better it is for your game.

A cardroom's only interest in the poker game is to provide a good environment so that their players enjoy the game and will keep playing and generating the rakes they make as their fees.

◆ PROTECTING YOUR CARDS ◆

If you watch a live game or tournament, you'll notice that some players keep a chip or small ornament on top of their cards when they play. These are called **card protectors**, and their purpose is to protect the hand from being fouled and declared invalid. If a dealer inadvertently takes your cards and they were not protected, your hand is considered dead or fouled, even though it may have been the dealer's mistake. Your cards are considered "live" and protected when there is a chip or ornament placed on top of them.

A hand is also considered fouled if you show your cards to the table or flip one over, if other cards somehow get commingled with them, or if the cards drop to the floor. In tricky situations, a supervisor will be called over to render a decision according to the rules of the cardroom.

♠ TRUTH BE BAD, LIES BE GOOD ♠

Strange but true. If you announce your cards before the showdown while a hand is in progress, your cards are considered dead if you are telling the truth. If, however, you are lying about their strength, then that's considered fair game—the cards are live!

---

6. THE BASICS OF HOLD'EM

All play and strategy in hold'em depends upon the position of the **button**, which is a small disk, typically plastic and labeled "Dealer." The player who has the button in front of him, who is also known as the button, will have the advantage of acting last in every round of betting except for the preflop round. After each hand is completed, the disk rotates clockwise to the next player.

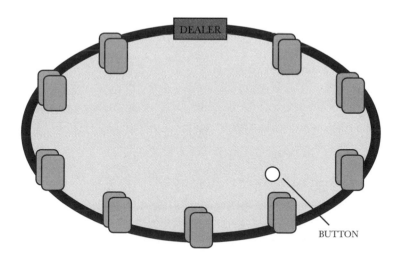

The player immediately to the left of the button is called the **small blind** and the one to his left is called the **big blind**.

These two players are required to post bets, called **blinds**, before the cards are dealt.

The big blind is typically the same size as the lower bet in a limit structure, so if you're in a $3/$6 game, the big blind would be $3 and in a $5/$10 game, it would be $5. The small blind will either be half the big blind in games where the big blind evenly divides to a whole dollar, or two-thirds of the big blind when it doesn't. For example, the small blind might be $2 in a $3/$6 game and $10 in a $15/$30 game.

In no-limit cash games, the amount of the blinds are preset and remain constant throughout the game. Typical blinds for cash games might be $2/$5, $3/$5 or $5/$10 for the small blind and big blind respectively. Bigger blinds mean more action and larger games.

In tournaments, however, the blinds steadily increase as the event progresses, forcing players to play boldly to keep up with the greater costs of these bets.

♦ ANTES ♦

Antes are mandatory bets that every player must make before the cards are dealt and are in addition to the blinds. They are only required in tournaments after some rounds have been played (see *Tournament Basics* chapter). There are no antes in cash hold'em games.

♠ Seating Arrangements

Around a poker table, seat 1 identifies the place to the immediate left of the dealer, seat 2 the chair to that player's left, and so on until seat 10, which would be immediately to the right of the dealer in a 10-player game. While players can be identified in relation to where the dealer sits, a player's *position* has an entirely different meaning.

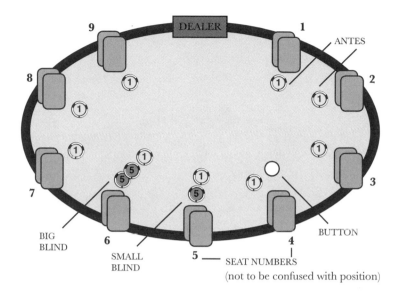

BIG BLIND   6   SMALL BLIND   5 —— SEAT NUMBERS
(not to be confused with position)

Position describes a player's relative position to the player acting last in a poker round. Thus, if the player in seat 5 is to bet first, he is in early position, and the player to his immediate right, who will act last since the action goes clockwise, will be in late position.

♦ ORDER OF BETTING ♦

Play always proceeds clockwise around the table. On the preflop, the first betting round, the first player to the left of the big blind goes first. He can call the big blind to stay in competition for the pot, raise, or fold. Every player following him has the same choices: call, raise, or fold.

The last player to act on the preflop is the big blind. If no raises have preceded his turn, the big blind can either end the betting in the round by calling—no further chips need to be put in since his blind bet has already been made—or he can put in a raise. However, if there are any raises in the round, the big blind and other remaining players must call or raise these bets to stay active, or they must fold.

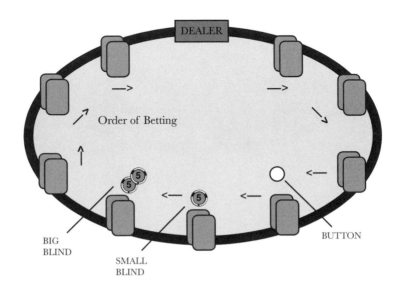

On the other betting rounds—the flop, turn and river—the first active player to the button's left will go first and the player on the button will go last. If the button has folded, the player sitting closest to his right will act last. When all bets and raises have been met on the flop and turn, or if all players check, then the next card will be dealt. On the river, after all betting action is completed, players will reveal their cards to see who has the best hand.

Betting in a round stops when the last bet or raise has been called and no bets or raises are due any player. Players cannot raise their own bets or raises.

At any time before the showdown, if all opponents fold, then the last active player wins the pot.

♠ **PLAYING TIP** ♠

Never fold the big blind unless the pot has been raised. If there is no raise, there is no cost to play and you can see the flop for free.

♦ SAMPLE GAME ♦

Let's follow the action in a sample $3/$6 limit game with nine players so that you can see how hold'em is played.

In limit poker, the betting structure has two levels, the lower levels being the amount you must bet or raise on the preflop and flop ($3 in a $3/$6 game), and the higher levels being the amount you must bet or raise on the turn and river ($6 in a $3/$6 game).

A no-limit game would proceed *exactly* like the sample limit hold'em game shown below—the same order of play and the same options are available to the players. The only difference is that there is no cap to the amount that can be bet. Players can bet or raise any amount greater than the minimum allowed, up to all their chips, when it is their turn.

Before the cards are dealt, the small blind and the big blind must post their bets. Once that occurs, the dealer will distribute cards one at a time, beginning with the small blind, who is the player sitting to the immediate left of the button, and proceeding clockwise until all players have received two face down cards.

♠ The Preflop

The player to the big blind's left acts first. He has the option of calling the $3 big blind bet, raising it $3 more, or folding. Checking is not an option on the preflop as there is already a bet on the table—the $3 big blind bet.

Let's say this player folds. The next player is faced with the same decisions: call, raise, or fold. He calls for $3. Since this is a $3/$6 game, all bets and raises in this round *must* be in $3 increments. The next three players fold. The following player raises $3, making it $6 total—the $3 call plus the $3 raise.

It is the button's turn, the player sitting in the dealer position. He thinks about his cards and calls the $6. Now it is up to the small blind. The small blind has already put in $2 so he must put in $4 more to play. If there had been no raise, it would cost him just $1 more to meet the $3 big blind bet and stay active—but that's not the case.

The small blind folds and the big blind considers reraising the raiser, but instead just calls the $3 raise. Play now moves back to the original caller. Since he has only put $3 into the pot, he must meet the $3 raise to stay in the hand. He calls and since all bets and raises have been matched, the round is over. We'll see the flop four-handed.

The big blind always has the option to raise on the preflop. If there had been no raises before the big blind's turn to act, then the dealer will ask the big blind if he wishes to raise by announcing "option." If the big blind just calls, the preflop betting is finished for the round. If the big blind exercises his option and raises, then the other active players must meet that raise to stay active.

If all players fold on the preflop, that is, there are no callers, then the big blind wins the hand by default.

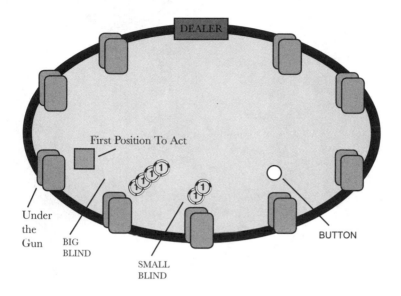

♠ The Flop

At the conclusion of betting, the dealer pulls the blinds and bets into the pot. He takes the top card off the deck and **burns** it, that is, he removes it from play, and then deals the three card flop face-up in the center of the table.

Bets and raises during this round are still at the $3 level. The first active player to the button's left goes first. Since the small blind has folded, it is the big blind's turn. There are no bets that have to be met—the forced first round blind bet only occurs on the preflop—so the big blind may check or bet. (There is no reason to fold, which would be foolish, as it costs nothing to stay active.)

The big blind checks, the next player checks, the original raiser from the preflop checks, and it is now up to the button. He pushes $3 into the pot forcing the other three players to put up $3 if they want to see another card. The big blind, who checked

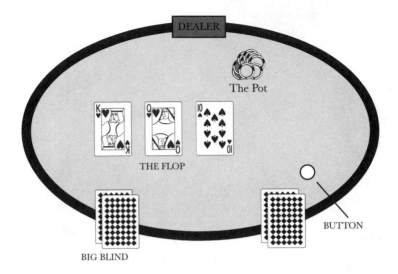

first in this round, is the next active player. He must call or raise this bet to continue with the hand, or he must fold. He decides to call for $3 and the other two players fold. Since all bets have been called, betting is complete for the round.

We're now heads-up, the big blind versus the button.

♠ The Turn

The dealer burns the top card and then deals a fourth community card face-up on the table. This is known as the **turn** or **fourth street**. Betting moves to the upper limit, so now all bets and raises are in $6 increments. The big blind, being the first active player on the button's left, goes first and checks. The button checks as well. Since all active players checked, the betting round is over.

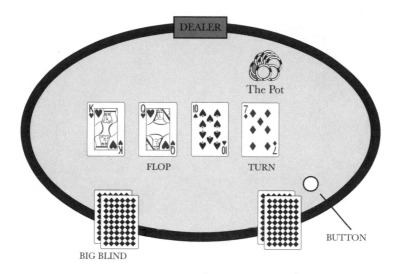

♠ The River and the Showdown

After the top card is burned, the fifth and final community card is turned over and placed next to the other four cards in the center of the table. Players now have five community cards along with their two pocket cards to form their final five card hand.

At the **river** or **fifth street**, there is one final round of betting. The big blind goes first and leads out with a $6 bet. The button calls, and that concludes the betting since the big blind cannot raise his own bet. We now have the showdown. The big blind turns over K-Q, which combines with a board of K-Q-10-7-5 for two pair of kings and queens. The button's K-10 also gives him two pair led by kings, but his second pair is tens. The big blind has the superior hand and wins the money in the pot.

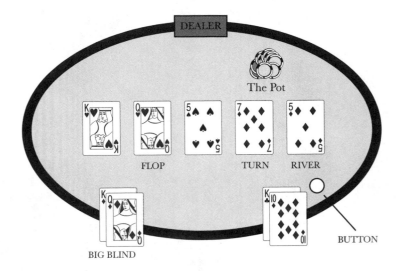

Had the button simply folded, the big blind would have won by default, since no other players remained to contest the pot.

On the showdown, the last player to bet or raise (or if there has been no betting in the round, then the first person to the left of the button) has to show his cards first. Losers can simply **muck** their cards, that is, fold them, without showing their cards.

The dealer pushes the chips in the pot over to the winner, collects and shuffles the cards, and prepares to deal a new hand. The button moves clockwise, so the big blind is now the small blind, and the small blind becomes the button.

♦ READING THE FLOP ♦

You only start with two cards, and to form certain hands, like straights, flushes, and full houses, your cards must connect with the board. Below are some examples that show how certain types of hands can be formed from the flop.

1. THE FLOP: THREE SUITED CARDS

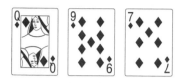

Biggest Possible Hand on This Flop: Flush

♠ What to Look Out For:

A flush can be made only if there are three suited cards on board. In this example, any player holding two diamonds would have a flush. If there were only two suited cards on board, no player could currently hold a made flush, though one could be formed later if a third flush card showed on board.

2. THE FLOP: TWO SUITED CARDS

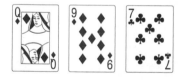

Biggest Possible Hand on This Flop: Three of a Kind

♠ What to Look Out For:

This flop is identical to the one previous, except that the last card, the seven, is a club. When the flop contains two suited cards, you know that an opponent will need a third suited card to complete the flush. An opponent may be drawing to a flush, but he cannot make one unless another diamond falls on the turn or river.

3. THE FLOP: THREE CONSECUTIVE CARDS

Biggest Possible Hand on This Flop: Straight

♠ What to Look Out For:

Any player holding J-10, 6-5, or 10-6 has flopped a straight. There are also straight draws out there for any player holding any J, 10, 6, or 5. If you hold a pair of tens, this flop is excellent. You have an overpair (a higher pair than any board card) and a straight draw. On the other hand, if you have a premium pair such as aces or kings, this flop is terrible. You have to worry about opponents cracking them with straights and straight draws.

4. THE FLOP: PAIR ON BOARD

Biggest Possible Hand on This Flop: Four of a Kind

♠ What to Look Out For:

Once a pair forms on board, three-of-a-kinds, full houses, and even quads are possible. Any player who holds K-J is seeing one of the prettiest flops he's ever seen (full house of jacks and kings)—but that's not quite as pretty as it is to a player holding two pocket kings for a bigger full house or a player holding two jacks for quads!

5. THE FLOP: CONSECUTIVE CARDS— TWO GAP

Biggest Possible Hand on This Flop: Straight

♠ What to Look Out For:

When there are no more than two gaps between the cards on board, it is possible that a player has flopped a straight. In this example, a player holding a 10-9 as pocket cards loves what he's looking at. Other two-gap flops include J-10-7 and J-9-7; one-gap flops include J-10-8 and J-9-8. If the flop has more than two gaps between the cards, it is impossible for any player to have made a straight. Thus, no player can have a straight if the flop comes J-8-6 (two gaps between the 9 and 10, and one gap between the 8-6).

♠ POSSIBLE HANDS FORMED BY THE BOARD ♠

Board Shows	Possible Hands
Three suited cards	Flush
Three consecutive cards (2 gaps or less)	Straight
Pair on board	Three of a kind, Full house

◆ HOW TO READ THE FLOP: THREE PRACTICE HANDS ◆

See if you can figure out the types of hands that can be formed from the flops below. Explanations are on the following pages.

FLOP ONE

FLOP TWO

FLOP THREE

◆ ANSWERS: THREE PRACTICE HANDS ◆

FLOP ONE

Best Hands by Rank	Player's Hole Cards
Straight flush spades	7♠ 6♠
Any flush	Any two spades with A♠ being the highest
Straight	7-6 in any suit, but not both spades
Three of a kind	9-9, 8-8, 5-5

♠ Key Points:

A flop of three suited cards (spades, in this example) means that any player holding two spades as pocket cards has a made flush. Forming a completed flush on the flop is impossible unless all three cards are suited. A straight is also possible because there are less than two gaps between the cards, but that would be a dangerous hand to play given the flush possibilities on board. And note the straight flush possibility!

FLOP TWO

Best Hands by Rank	Player's Hole Cards
Three of a kind	J-J, 10-10, 6-6
Two pair	J-10, J-6, 10-6,
Pair	A-A, K-K, Q-Q, J-any

♠ Key Points:

Without three suited cards, no flush is possible. And with the flop being **rainbow**, all different suits, there is no flush draw to be concerned with. Neither is there a made straight draw, as the flop has more than two gaps. The best hand any player can currently hold is a set (three of a kind).

FLOP THREE

Best Hands by Rank	Player's Hole Cards
Four of a kind	Q-Q
Full house	Q-10, 10-10
Three of a kind	Q-x (x - any card other than a 10)
Two pair	A-A, K-K, 10-x (x- any card other than Q)

♠ Key Points:

A pair on the board makes a full house possible, as well as a rare four-of-a-kind hand. Whenever a pair flops, it is impossible for any player to have made a completed flush or straight. In this example, a player with two clubs would have a flush draw, and a straight draw would be possible with any of these combinations: A-J, K-J, K-9, J-9, and J-8. These draws would need a good card to come on the turn or river to complete, but a player going for a straight should be concerned about a third club falling. And everyone on a draw knows that a full house is possible.

♦ HOW TO READ THE BOARD: FOUR PLAYERS ♦

In the following example, you will see all five board cards. See if you can figure out the best hand held by each player.

PLAYER A

PLAYER B

PLAYER C

PLAYER D

THE BOARD

♦ ANSWERS: THE BEST HANDS, FOUR PLAYERS ♦

♠ The Hands Formed:

Player A	Two pair: aces and fives
	A♣ A♦ 5♥ 5♦ K♣
Player B	Two pair: nines and fives
	9♥ 9♦ 5♥ 5♦ J♥
Player C	Full house: fives full of aces
	5♥ 5♦ 5♣ A♦ A♥
Player D	Flush: diamond flush
	9♦ A♦ 5♦ 6♦ 7♦

♠ The Best Hands

Going into the river, Player C was leading with two pair, aces and fives, but there was danger. Diamond and heart flush draw were possible, and Player C did not want to see either one of those suits come on the river card. And indeed, two players, Player B and Player D were on flush draws. In fact, Player D was on both a flush draw *and* an inside straight draw, needing any diamond to complete the flush and an 8 to make a straight. If that 8 was a diamond, the hand would be a monster—a straight flush! Player A picked up aces on the turn, but like Player C, had to feel nervous about those flush draws.

The river does bring another diamond, making a diamond flush possible. While Player A improves to two pair, aces and fives, he is doomed by the flush made by Player D. And Player B also makes two pair, but those fives, being on board, helped Player A much more as the aces and fives are stronger than the nines and fives. Player B would have preferred a heart to make the flush, but only as long as that heart didn't make a full house for an opponent!

Player D got his diamond, but a dangerous diamond it was. It paired the board, making a full house—a stronger hand—possible. And sure enough, Player C completes his full house, catching a beautiful 5♦ to take the pot.

7. YOUR FIRST TIME IN A CARDROOM

If it's your first time in a cardroom or playing in a tournament—or among your first times—you're probably going to be a little nervous. That's okay, it's natural to have a small case of the jitters. However, once you sit down, settle in, and get acclimated, you'll soon find your environment to be friendly and comfortable.

Even though players vigorously compete for each other's money, the typical poker game is a social and friendly affair, regardless of the stakes played. That goes for a $1/$2 game, as well as the "big game," where the best players in the world—Doyle Brunson, Johnny Chan, Chip Reese, Phil Ivey, and Barry Greenstein—throw friendly barbs at one another while millions of dollars in chips move around the table. This friendly environment prevails equally at $20 buy-in tournament tables to big championship events that cost $10,000, or even $25,000, to enter.

So if you miss a few opportunities in the first 30 minutes or so, it's no big deal. There is no rush to get involved in a major hand. Do not make the mistake of forcing action if you are not ready. You'll lose a ton of chips because you weren't adjusted to the environment. Take it easy, there's lots of play ahead.

Sedatives such as valium and alcohol might calm your nerves, but they also impair your judgment, so I strongly advise against using them. Over time, you'll get used to your surroundings and be able to turn on your best play. So don't sweat it.

♠ Cardrooms Are Widely Available

Thanks to the massive surge of interest in poker, public cardrooms offering poker games are more readily found today than in any time in the past. Poker rooms are almost *de rigueur* in most casinos, and if you can't find a legal game, there's sure to be underground and semi-private games available. Gigantic poker rooms dot southern California, in particular the Bicycle Casino in Bell Gardens and the Commerce Club in Commerce. With the worldwide growth in popularity, finding poker rooms around the globe is no longer a Herculean odyssey. And of course, there is the Internet, in which poker games are available virtually anywhere you have a phone line and access to a computer.

But in this chapter, we'll concentrate on how to play in the physical poker rooms where you sit across from your opponents in a public or semi-public setting.

♦ PLAYING YOUR FIRST CASH GAME ♦

Big cardrooms typically offer a choice of hold'em (limit, no-limit, and perhaps pot-limit games), and various forms of seven card stud and Omaha. There might be other games available as well, depending on the setting. Nowadays though, if you find poker being spread, you can pretty much be assured that there are hold'em games available to play.

If the poker room is popular and you arrive during the prime-time hours (evenings and weekends), you might wait as long as several hours for a seat. Yes, poker is *that* popular.

When you enter into a poker room, you'll need to go directly to the sign-up area so you can register. The **poker host** will ask you which games and limits you prefer and put you on the list.

Usually the poker host will take your first name and last initial, or just both initials. And then you just have to wait. It is first-come, first-served, so to avoid the longer waits, get there early if you know you're going to playing in prime times. Some rooms take reservations, so check before you arrive: you may even be able to call in advance to reserve a seat. A good old-fashioned tip of a sufficient amount can work wonders, but that of course, is at your discretion.

If you plan on stepping out for a bite or a smoke, tell the poker host to **lock** your seat, and that will buy you extra time.

When your name is called, you will either be directed to your seat by a **floorman**—in some clubs, a small tip is customary—or told the table and seat number.

In a larger room, you'll have all sorts of choices, from $1-$4 or $1-$5 spread-limit games, to $3/$6 games, on up to tables that may spread $100/$200 games or higher. Check into the poker room at the Bellagio Casino in Las Vegas and you might find a game dealing $2,000/$4,000 (or higher if you want to push the players to bigger limits), but you'd be sitting with the most famous and best players in poker.

♠ Getting Chips

Once you're seated, you'll need chips. That task will be taken care of by a **chip runner**, whose job is to take your buy-in and return with the proper equivalent in chips. There is usually a minimum buy-in required, but it is always reasonable and appropriate to the limit you'll be playing. Also, you never want to buy in for less anyway—you'd have too few chips to play a reasonable game.

Any time that you run out of chips and need to buy more, you simply alert the dealer, and he will summon the chip runner—or you can call for him yourself.

♠ Joining a Game in Progress

If you're joining a game in progress and your seat has just been bypassed by the blind, you'll often be required to post a blind bet on your first hand or you'll be given a choice to wait out the action until the big blind gets to you. If you post the big blind early, you'll enjoy the same privileges as the actual big blind—a free look at the flop unless there has been a raise, in which case you must call those extra chips in order to play. The advantage of waiting is that it allows you to watch the game and get comfortable for a few hands before your play. Don't worry about the details—the dealer will fill you in on your choices and what is required.

If you have any questions about blinds or any other aspect of the rules or procedures, just ask the dealer. It is his or her job to keep you informed.

♠ Taking Breaks

It is perfectly fine to take breaks from the table. Just let the dealer know you'll be taking some time and he'll hold the seat for you, usually up to 30 minutes or so. In a major cardroom, it is customary to leave your chips at the table; they'll be watched by the dealer and respected by the other players.

♠ Changing Seats

In a cash game, if you find your seat to be unlucky or in a bad strategic spot given the strength or type of players on either side of you, you can change to any other seat at the table should one open up. In a tournament, however, you have no such right. It is the luck of the draw where you are assigned, and you are not allowed to move.

♦ PLAYING YOUR FIRST TOURNAMENT ♦

At some point, you'll want to get your feet wet and get involved in the very exciting world of tournament poker. There is too much money to be made in the tournament games—and too much fun to be had—that it would be a shame for you not to play.

Are you a little nervous about what to do? Don't be! We'll go over the basics and you'll see there's not much to worry about. Just find out where the tournaments are, pay your entry fee, grab a seat, and play!

To get started in a tournament, you have to register and pay the entrance fee. The sign-up area is usually in the poker room. Otherwise, signs, the poker room employees, or fellow players will let you know where you can get registered. You will often be required to show an I.D., especially in the big events, so make sure to bring that along when you go to register.

Some of the big tournaments held in casinos require you to use casino chips as your buy-in—you may not use cash at the buy-in area—so make sure to ask in the tournament areas *before* you end up unnecessarily running around chasing chips and entry fees because you weren't aware of this requirement. If this is the case, simply go to a casino cage and exchange cash for chips, which you will then exchange at the registration area for your entry.

The sign-up process is pretty easy. All you do is fill out a form and hand over the entrance fee. In return, you'll get a slip of paper assigning you to a table and seat where you will begin play at the allotted time. When you sit down to play, you show the dealer your receipt. Unlike a cash game, you *cannot* change seats. The only possible exception is if two family members or husband and wife are at the same table, and then it would be up to the tournament director to make changes.

♠ Registering Early

In major tournaments, especially the World Series of Poker held every year, huge lines form hours before the tournament is scheduled to begin. In order to avoid the hassles of a tournament that attracts hundreds of players—and in the case of the World Series, thousands of players—make sure to register well in advance. You can usually register up to a week or two before the event on the premises—and sometimes much earlier.

If you do come late, there is no penalty other than the chips you'd lose to the blinds once the tournament begins. This is not a huge loss as the blinds are small for the first few levels of play, but it is better to get acclimated as the tournament begins rather than come in late, feeling rushed and out of sync.

In smaller tournaments, there is usually no problem coming last minute as the field is smaller and the tournament personnel have enough resources to get you signed up easily. And the process is even more informal at these small tournaments. Try to get there at least 15 minutes before the scheduled start time. Even better, give yourself 30 minutes. You'll have a good time chatting it up with the other players while you wait for the first cards to be dealt.

♠ The Major Tournaments

The big poker event that is center of all poker players' dreams and aspirations is the World Series of Poker. It is held every summer in Las Vegas. The main event, the $10,000 buy-in no-limit hold'em championship is the one that crowns the world champion. But the World Series is more than just the "big one;" it is actually a series of over 40 events, each of which awards a gold bracelet, a championship title for the event, and bragging rights to the winner—plus a big first-place cash prize! Most of the events are no-limit hold'em events of various buy-ins ranging from $1,000 to $10,000, but there are also limit and pot-limit hold'em, seven-card stud, Omaha, some form of draw poker (lowball, triple draw), and events that combine multiple games. In all, the championships span more than six weeks, with the main event taking more than ten days to conclude.

The WSOP has also started a series of major tournaments held around the country in various locales, which are considered important events for the pros.

The main credit for the resurgence and popularity of poker goes to two visionary men—Steve Lipscomb and Lyle Berman—who together formed the World Poker Tour and brought high-stakes tournament play into the living room of America and the world. The World Poker Tour events are considered by poker players to be the second-most prestigious set of tournaments, after the World Series championships. There are more than 15 WPT events that crown champions. Most of the tournaments take place in the Unites States, but events are also held in Paris, the Bahamas, Aruba, and even one on a cruise ship.

See www.cardozapub.com for a listing of the tournament events.

♠ More on Tournament Play

See the *Tournament Basics* chapter for full coverage of tournament play.

♦ OTHER RULES AND PROCEDURES ♦

The following rules and procedures apply to both cash games and tournaments.

♠ Disputes

Various disputes can arise during a game, either between players, or between a player and the dealer. It his occurs, ask the dealer to call over the "floor," meaning the floorman, or call out for him yourself. Disputes are handled according to the procedures of the cardroom, and the floorman, will always follow the rules and try to be fair when interpretations are required.

♠ A Word on Smoking

Smoking is typically not allowed in public poker rooms in the United States, so if you're a smoker, you'll have to head to the public areas of the cardroom or outside to get your puffs in.

♠ Asking for Time

You are allowed to take extra time—up to a reasonable limit—during the play of a hand, a privilege you may want to use if you're faced with a difficult decision. Your opponents remedies for undue deliberation, as well as yours if an opponent takes too long to make a decision, is to ask for the "clock." When a clock is called, the floorman will come over and give the deliberating player 60 seconds in which to make a decision, or his hand will automatically be folded. Any player at the table may call for the clock, even one not actively involved in the hand. When ten seconds remain, the floorman will countdown from ten so that the clocked player has advance warning that his time will expire.

8. SEVEN KEY STRATEGIC CONCEPTS

The following key concepts apply to all forms of hold'em, and for that matter, all forms of poker.

1. Reading Your Opponents

2. Be Aggressive

3. Respect Position

4. Play Strong Starting Cards

5. Win Chips, Not Pots

6. Fold When You're Beat

7. Have Patience

We'll look at each concept in turn, beginning with the two most important.

1. READING YOUR OPPONENTS

Poker is a game of cards played against people. How opponents react to your betting actions, and you to theirs, determines who is going to win and who is going to lose. In the long run, every player is going to get the same number of good cards and bad cards. It is how you play the cards you're dealt that determines if you're going to walk away with more chips than you started. And how you play those cards is determined by the opponents you're playing against. To win, you must play your opponents wisely, adjusting to their strengths and taking advantage of their weaknesses.

By watching how an opponent plays, you get all sorts of information on how to take advantage of his tendencies. For example, when a player infrequently enters a pot, he's **tight**, and you can often force him out of hands by making bets and raises, even when he may have better cards than you. You'll give him credit for big hands when he's in a pot, and get out of his way unless you have a big hand yourself.

On the other hand, an opponent who plays a lot of hands is **loose**, and you can figure him for weaker cards on average. You also need to adjust for **aggressive** players, who often raise when they get involved in a pot, and **passive** players, who you can play against with less fear of getting raised.

There is a lot to learn to become a better poker player, but to a great degree, improving your game depends on you becoming a better people-reader. When you understand the tendencies and playing styles of your opponents, you can formulate a plan on how to outmaneuver and defeat them.

There are two traits that define a winning poker player. The first is an ability to read opponents. It is so important that I've devoted an entire chapter, *Playing the Player*, to a broader discussion on how to adjust your strategies to take advantage of your opponents' tendencies and weaknesses.

The second trait, which is a running theme of this book, we'll turn to now.

2. AGGRESSION

The best hold'em players share one common trait—aggression. When they're in a hand, they put the action to their opponents by either betting when they act first or when an opponent checks to them, or raising when it's bet to them. They make their opponents make tough decisions. And if you want to elevate your game, you need to do the same.

Betting when there are no bets due and raising when there are puts pressure on opponents and forces them to commit more chips in order to stay in competition for the pot. One big advantage of aggressive play is that it often causes opponents to fold, giving you a "free" pot without having to face a showdown. When this occurs, you have a 100% chance of winning, and you can't beat that percentage. Aggressive play also allows you to narrow the field or isolate opponents.

Being heads-up gives you a much better shot of winning a pot than playing against three or more players. Now, you have only one person to beat. If two opponents enter pots with hands of equal strength and play about the same way, you can expect similar results. With all else equal, you have a fifty-fifty shot of winning. Of course, all else will not always be equal. But in the long run, if you're heads-up and push at an opponent with another bet, your chances of winning increase because you increase the likelihood that he will fold and give up the pot. Aggressive play shifts the odds. In a pot, the bettor or raiser is the favorite for exactly that reason.

As you can see, aggressive betting makes the math start looking better. Your opponents become more cautious, you get more free cards when you want them, your opponents fold more often when you bet, and they become more reluctant to lead out against you because they know you might raise them right back. Best of all, aggressive betting makes your opponents more predictable, giving you a clearer picture of how to proceed when they play back at you.

Whenever you put pressure on opponents, it gives you the strength and your opponents the fear. Aggressive play lets you set the tempo of the game and forces opponents to play at *your* pace.

3. RESPECT POSITION

In hold'em, where you sit relative to the button is called **position**. In a nine-handed game, the first three spots to the left of the button are known as **early position**, the next three, **middle position**, and the last three, **late position**. In a ten-handed game, early position is the four spots to the left of the button.

The later your position, the bigger your advantage, because you get to see what your opponents do before deciding whether to commit any chips to the pot. Position is extremely critical in hold'em because it is maintained for four betting rounds—the preflop, flop, turn and river. If you have later position than opponents, this advantage becomes a significant weapon that you can use to bully players who must act before you. On the other hand, the earlier your position, the more vulnerable your hand is to being raised and thus the more powerful your hand must be for you to enter the pot.

For example, say you just call the big blind from early position with a mediocre hand, hoping to get in cheap to see the flop. If an opponent raises and your hand is not strong enough to call, you have cost yourself chips. This is particularly true in no-limit and pot-limit games where the raise could be for a lot of chips. If you **limp** (call as opposed to raise) too often and are pushed out of pots by aggressive raisers, you'll lose lots of chips without getting the benefit of seeing additional cards for your bet!

Thus, position is a factor when deciding whether you should play a pair of twos or a pair of jacks, and whether you should bet, raise, or fold. In the long run, you'll play more hands and have better results from late position than from middle or early position because your advantage is greater. More options and leverage means more success—more chips—and that is what position is all about. Let's take the starting cards of K-Q. You're first to act in a no-limit game and let's say you limp into the pot.

A tight player after your position raises. If you call that raise, you're probably an underdog to a better hand, so you throw the cards away. You've just lost chips because you left yourself vulnerable in early position. If you keep playing vulnerable hands that can't stand raises from early position, then you're going to lose too many chips. And if you defend weaker hands against raises, your chip losses will be even worse.

If you're in late position, then it's a different story. You have more options and leverage so you can play more hands. If the early betting action is aggressive, you can fold marginal hands without cost. And if the betting action is weak, you can be more aggressive with marginal hands and see the flop with better position. You can decide if that K-Q is worth a further bet based upon seeing the action around the table before it gets to you. If there is a big raise before you, you can throw your K-Q to the wind without any cost. And if you think the hand is worth some chips, you can enter the pot with less risk of being raised. And that makes a very big difference.

♠ TIP ♠

As a general rule in any form of hold'em, you need stronger hands to play up front and weaker hands from the back. For example, if all players have folded to you on the button, you can play weaker hands since the only threats of raises behind you are the two blinds—who, if they do play with you, will be out of position on the next three betting rounds.

4. PLAY STRONG STARTING CARDS

Starting out with good cards gives you the best chance of winning. While this may seem obvious, you'd be surprised at the number of players who ignore this basic strategic concept and take loss after loss by chasing inferior and losing hands. If you play too many hands in poker, you'll soon find yourself without chips. Enter the pot with good starting cards in the right position and you'll have a good chance of finishing with winners.

Sometimes you're dealt playable starting cards; more often, you're not. In the first case, you play the good hands and see where they take you. But in the second instance, where your cards are not promising and you're a big underdog, folding is the proper strategy.

You don't want to give away bets. The preflop is where you make the decision of whether or not to play the hand at all. If you decide to play, do you want to get in and see the flop cheaply? Or do you want to try to win the pot right on the spot with an intimidating bet? As you begin to play no-limit, you'll notice a very curious thing: the majority of pots are won right on the preflop, when one player raises and everyone else folds.

In limit poker, multiple players often see the flop since the entry fee into the pot is smaller, but this doesn't change the basic idea: don't go into that pot without cards that either are favored to win, or if they are weaker, at least give you a good price to chase.

You can't win every hand and you shouldn't try. Be judicious with the hands you choose to play. Hands that start strong tend to end strong. And hands that start weak tend to end weak. Of course, strong hands may die on the vine, and weak ones can turn into big hands, but if you continually play speculative hands hoping they'll draw big, you're going to lose a lot of chips.

5. WIN CHIPS, NOT POTS

Many novice players have a misconception that winning more pots equates to being a bigger winner at the tables. In fact, the opposite is true! Aggressive weak players tend to win more pots than stronger players because they're playing too many hands. Naturally, the more hands you play to the end, the more hands you will win, but that doesn't necessarily lead to more profits. Every pot contested comes at a cost. When you contest many and lose many, it leads to a mighty bad day.

Your goal is to win money, not pots. There is a significant difference between the two. After all, at the end of a poker session, you're not going to measure your results by how many pots you won, but by how much money you won or lost. Winning money is what counts in poker—the final result.

It is not the quantity of pots you win, but the *quality* of them that matters. When you've got a big hand, you want to extract as many chips from your opponents as you can. Many beginning players make the mistake of pushing opponents out of hands in which they could have extracted more chips by betting too high, forcing their opponents to immediately fold. This doesn't mean you should not aggressively bet your big hands. On the contrary, you need to protect hands that are strong by betting aggressively. But be aware that sometimes you can extract more chips from opponents by allowing them to see another card, or in no-limit, by making bets that opponents feel compelled to call, even though they think they've got the worst of it in a hand.

Of course, the problem with betting strong hands weakly, called **slowplaying**, is that you don't get big hands very often. If you're in a tournament, you may only see a situation like that once or twice in a day. Perhaps not at all. But in the meantime, you've got to earn chips by being aggressive in the right situations, and by baiting opponents into pots you're likely to win in others.

No matter how you play a hand, don't lose sight of the basic premise: winning chips.

6. FOLD WHEN YOU'RE BEAT

Winning money in poker is not just about winning pots. In fact, being an overall winning player has more to do with losing *less* when your cards don't come in the running than winning big when you have the best hand! Many players don't appreciate this concept. They might win enough pots, get enough good hands, yet they can't understand why they keep leaving the table with losses or marginal wins.

Folding when you're beaten is one of the most important concepts in poker. For example, let's say you're dealt pocket aces, the best possible starting hand in hold'em. You bring it in for a raise from early position, and get two callers. On the flop, three spades fall and you have none of it. You bet, there is a raise by the second player, and then a reraise by the third player.

You're facing potential flushes, and given all this action, your pocket rockets may be a huge underdog. If you call, you might get reraised again, perhaps with an all-in bet (if you're playing no-limit). Either way, this is a potential going home hand. And if a straight draw such as 7-8-9 falls, or a pair forms on board and you don't have a piece of it (particularly a high pair that is more dangerous since opponents are more likely to hold high cards than low cards), your aces may be up against trips.

Even if you have aces heads-up, there are times you have to recognize that there is too much strength out there and you may be beat. Sure, aces start strong, but once the flop falls, you always need to reevaluate.

♠ ESSENTIAL CONCEPT ♠

It is as important to make good folds in poker as it is to make good bets.

More money is lost by players who consistently make bet after bet in clearly losing situations than in possibly any other facet of poker. Every extra bet you contribute to an opponent's pot is one more bet out of your stack. To be a winner at poker, you must hold your money dear and value it as if it were gold. There are good bets in poker, and there are bad bets. If you can cut the number of your bad bets in half, you'll turn losing sessions into winning sessions and small winning sessions into larger winning sessions.

Do not play with cards that cannot win. Never lose sight of this concept when you're playing. When you lose, you should lose on hands you thought would be winners or which gave you good odds to play out as an underdog. Never lose with hands on which your odds of winning aren't worth the bets you're making; you shouldn't even be playing these cards.

Folding losing hands will make you more money at poker in the long run than any other strategic aspect of the game. In fact, it is *essential* if you're going to be a winning player. Getting rid of weak hands should not be interpreted as advice to play like a rock, exit pots just because your hand is a dog, or bet only when you're in the lead. Far from it. Smart poker play means balancing bets with your chances of winning, and that includes playing for pots when you're strong, when you're trailing, and sometimes—given the right pot odds or the right opponent—when you're weak.

Your goal in poker must be to win money. Having constant action and being part of every pot will rapidly drain your bankroll. By definition, it means you're playing in too many pots, with too many inferior hands, for too long. This is not a winning strategy. Learning to recognize when you're beat or a big underdog in a situation will save you more chips than you can imagine.

7. PATIENCE

Hold'em is a game of patience. You will often go long stretches between good hands. Winning players exercise patience and wait for situations where they can win chips. Your good hands will come, and if you haven't blown yourself out trying to force plays—and are still around with chips in your pile—you'll be able to take advantage of them and win some nice pots for yourself. Quoting poker author and publisher Dana Smith, "You have to be in it, to win it." Too many players, itching to get some kind of action going, will stick their necks out with bets in inadvisable situations, and get their stacks destroyed.

Tournaments, even more than cash games, require patience. Lots of it. In a tournament, the first few rounds are all about waiting for opportunities. The blind and ante bets are minimal, so there is no hurry to force play. There is lots of time to let good situations develop. Many novices make the terrible mistake of pushing too hard, too early, when there is no reason to risk their tournament lives on foolish plays. When the blinds get high enough to hurt your stack or when you feel the right opportunity has come along, then it's time to play more aggressively. Other than that, think of yourself as a lion on the hunt. Just sit and wait; the right prey will come along.

In a tournament, as you approach the money, patience is more important than ever. You must wait for your situations, but not so long that you lose too much of your stack to the steady march of the blinds. When an opportunity presents itself, strike hard and try to build some chips, because if you can hang around long enough, you'll get over the bubble and into the money. And then you can set your sights higher.

9. RISKS AND REWARDS

Anytime you're contemplating risking money on a hand—that is, putting chips into the pot—the real question is, "Will it make me money?" If you can determine that the risk is worth the reward—that the bet will give you profits in the long run—then it is a good play. And if the play is not profitable in the long run, then it isn't a good play.

Poker players use two tools to get a handle on this: pot odds and implied odds. First of all, don't get intimidated by the complicated-sounding terms, which, upon your initial glance, may make you want to stick your head under a pillow and groan. I'm going to make the concepts easy to digest. So take the pillow away. You already use some form of these concepts all the time though you might not realize it! When you choose to go to a movie, you do so because you believe it will be worth your time and money. And when you buy a car, a house, or a collectible—really any purchase at all—you always ask yourself if the item is worth the cost.

It is the same in poker.. If a play will make money in the long run, you make the play, and if not, you don't. While you never really know exactly where you stand on a hand when you're contesting a pot, or how much money might end up in the pot by the time all the betting is complete, you can make educated guesses. You determine if it is worth putting more money in the pot based on your perceived chances of winning and the reward you would get if you prevail. In other words, is it a good bet?

Every time you're faced with a betting decision, try to get a sense of whether or not you've got the best hand. If you feel you don't, decide whether or not the money you'll have to invest in the pot is worth the amount of money you might win should your cards come home. Put simply: risk versus reward. In the long run, will you make money?

So how do you determine if a play is profitable? How do you know when the risk of putting more chips into the pot is worth the reward?

If you feel you have the best hand, it's a no-brainer—you always want more money in the pot. But if you feel your hand needs to improve to win, then you want to be aware of your chances of improving to a winner. All discussions of pot odds and implied odds start with a basic question: how many chances do you have to win? Poker players use a concept called "outs" to determine this.

Let's look at that now.

♦ OUTS ♦

Outs are the cards that will make your hand strong enough to win. For example, if you are all-in with two kings against an opponent with two aces and there is one card to come, you know you have two outs—the two remaining kings. No other card that comes on the river will improve your hand to a winner.

But unless you're all-in with your opponent, you'll never really know how many outs you have because you won't be able to see your opponent's cards. So calculating outs is not an exact science. But you do know your own cards and can easily determine your chances of improving to a stronger hand. And you can get a sense of where an opponent might be with his cards, based on how the betting is going and your knowledge of his play.

For example, say you have J♣ 10♣ and the board is A♣ 8♣ 7♥ 3♦.

YOU   **YOUR OPPONENT**

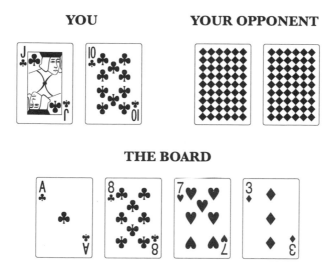

THE BOARD

On the turn, your opponent bets into you. You figure him for aces, perhaps a high pocket pair, hands you'll easily beat if you get another club to fill your flush draw. However, if you don't improve, you appear to have almost no chance of winning. After all, what can your unpaired J-10 beat? Not much. And if you pair your J or 10 on the river, you'd still be second best to all sorts of hands. You figure to need a club to win. There are nine clubs remaining in the deck, so you have nine outs.

THE REMAINING CLUBS

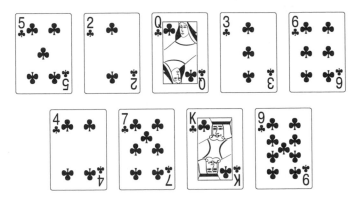

YOUR NINE OUTS

♦ WHAT ARE YOUR WINNING CHANCES? ♦

You know six cards, your two pocket cards and the four on the board. Since the deck has 52 cards, that leaves 46 unknown cards. Nine of those cards—the nine remaining clubs of the original 13 in the deck (you have two of those clubs and the board has two)—will improve your flush draw to a winner. The remaining 37 cards will lose. So the math is simple: 37 ways to lose, 9 ways to win (37 to 9), or a little more than 4 to 1 against with just one card to come.

Obviously, you're more likely to lose with this hand than win, and based on that alone, you'd never make the call. But there is another factor to consider: how many chips can you win? There is a reason people play the lottery even though they have almost no chance of winning and why poker players make calls and bets, even though they're an underdog to win the pot. And that reason is the *payoff*.

So is it worth calling the bet to see more cards? To answer

this question, we need to see if the payoff is good enough, and if it is, then it's worth calling the bet.

Now we turn to pot odds and implied odds to get our answer.

♦ POT ODDS ♦

Pot odds is the amount of money in the pot *including* what your opponent has already bet—because that money is in the pot, and he can't take it back—against what it will cost you to call the bet. For example, if $50 is in the pot, and you need to call a bet of $10 to play, you are getting pot odds of 5 to 1. So, in this situation, you can win $50. The question is: are your winning chances better than 5 to 1, which would be giving you good pot odds and make this a good bet, or worse than 5 to 1, which would be giving you bad pot odds and make this a bad bet?

In the earlier example where we had J-10, we determined that we had about a 4 to 1 chance of getting a club on the river. So with a payoff of 5 to 1 in a situation where it is only 4 to 1 against making the club flush, it is a good bet to make.

Let's look at another situation. Suppose there's $300 is in the pot and your opponent bets the size of the pot, another $300. Now there is $600 available to be won. It will cost you $300 to see the raise and have a chance to win that $600, so you are getting pot odds of 2 to 1. If you're on a flush draw or straight draw with one card to come and are figuring your hand to be about a 4 to 1 underdog, you are not getting enough of a return to make this a profitable call. On the other hand, if you figure your hand has about an even-money chance of winning, then you're getting great odds to make the call.

Here's another way to look at pot odds: let's say you are offered a proposition where you would bet $20 on a coin toss but could only win a total of only $1. You'd turn it down! You'd be getting incorrect odds—and how! The risk isn't worth the reward. However, if you would get $20 for every win, you'd have an even-money shot—a fair proposition. But if you could win $40 on that same flip of the coin, then you'd be very happy to risk $20 to win $40. You have one chance in two of winning (1 to 1 odds)—the same as on the other two propositions—but you would be getting a 2 to 1 payoff. If you made this bet all day long, you would make a fortune, provided your host didn't wise up or run out of money.

You use pot odds to determine if going for the pot is justified by the amount you might win. If the bet will make you money in the long run, it's a good bet. Whenever you have a hand that is favored to win, the pot odds will always be favorable. But it is also correct to play hands even though you are *not* favored to win—provided there is enough of a payoff for the risk.

When you do play second-best hands, it should be because they give you good value, because your long term expectation is to win money in that particular situation. You may be an underdog in a hand, but if, in the long term, playing it gives you more profits than losses, you should play it. If the situation is ripe for a bluff and that might take down the pot, there is good value in betting or raising with a weaker hand. Your opponent may not fold, but if you estimate that he will fold enough times to make aggressive betting profitable in that type of situation, it's a good play. Playing only good hands will make you predictable and playing too many bad hands will bury you in losses. Profitable play requires you to strike a balance between the two extremes.

But there is one more element you need to consider. What if there is more betting to come in the hand, especially if you're playing no-limit and have a chance to get an opponent for lots of chips?

Aha—now there's a key concept.

♦ POTENTIAL GAIN (IMPLIED ODDS) ♦

The amount *currently in the pot* (pot odds) is one thing, the amount that *might get into the pot* with further betting is another thing altogether. This concept is commonly called **implied odds**, though **potential gain** is an appropriate term as well, as the amount that might get into the pot is not implied but speculated.

By incorporating the concept of potential gain into your thinking, you increase the number of hands you might play in any form of poker but particularly in no-limit because of the large amount of chips that can be won in a pot. Whenever you play a hand, you must always consider the amount you stand to gain if you hit your cards and can induce an opponent to continue further into the hand—or he induces you, where, on that side of the coin, you need to figure out your risk! For example, in a tournament, if an opponent's stack is $5,000, you may consider that potential gain to be worth a certain amount of risk. On the other hand, if his stack is just $1,000, or if it is say $20,000, that may make a big difference in how you play your cards in a given situation.

So if a pot currently has $50 in it and you have a shot at getting $500 more by sneaking in there with a longshot hand and hitting it, it would be profitable to play more cards in the right circumstances. In other words, the cost is cheap and your hand would have a surprise value if it hit the board, giving you a chance to get lots of chips out of an opponent who couldn't accurately guess the strength of your cards—that is, in poker talk, he *couldn't put you on a hand*.

♦ OUTS AND CHANCES OF WINNING ♦

We've shown what happens on the turn with one card to come. What happens when you have that flush draw on the flop with two cards to come? Or if you have more or less outs? Where do you stand?

Luckily, there is simple formula that will allow you to figure your winning chances when you know the number of outs. I call this **Cardoza's 4 & 2 Rule**. On the turn, where there is only one card to come, you multiply the number of outs by two for a reasonable estimate of your chances of winning. And on the flop, where you have *two* cards to come, you multiply the number of outs by four.

These are not exact calculations, nor do they need to be. You just need to know *approximately* where you stand. Since the concept of outs is an educated estimate and not a perfect calculation anyway (because you can never be completely sure of the strength of your opponent's cards), exact figures are irrelevant.

And for this purpose, multiplying by two or four shows you about where you're at.

♠ CARDOZA'S 4 & 2 RULE ♠
ESTIMATING YOUR WINNING CHANCES

Betting Round	Multiply Outs by:
The Flop	4
The Turn	2

So if you have the same flush draw as in our earlier example, you have about an 18% chance of winning with one card to come, which we'll further simplify by rounding it up to a 20% chance of hitting your hand—again, a reasonable enough estimation to guide you along. If you had a flush draw on the flop, you'd multiply the 9 outs by 4, giving you about a 36% chance of winning, or roughly 1 chance in 3. Again, to make it simpler, we round it off to 35%. (Incidentally, the odds of making a flush are 36.4% and 20.5%, respectively, on the flop and turn, so you see we're pretty close using these estimates.)

Below is a chart that shows the number of outs you have for straight and flush draws.

♠ CHANCES OF COMPLETION: STRAIGHT AND FLUSH DRAWS ♠

Hand	Example	Outs	FLOP Approx. Odds of Filling	TURN Approx. Odds of Filling
Straight Draw	5♣6♥7♠8♣	8 outs	3 to 1	4 to 1
Flush Draw	Q♦9♦7♦3♦	9 outs	3 to 1	4 to 1

♦ SUMMING UP ♦

Any time the betting action is to you, make sure that the amount of money you invest will show a long term profit for you, meaning that the pot odds or the potential gain give you a healthy return on your investment of chips. If you quickly add up your outs, you'll have a sense of your winning chances.

10. LIMIT HOLD'EM STRATEGY

In limit hold'em, where all betting is in a two-tier structure, such as $3/$6 or $5/$10, the three main factors to consider when deciding how to play a hand are the strength of your starting cards, where you are sitting relative to the button, and the action that precedes your play. There are other considerations that enter into the mix, such as the cost of entering the pot and the aggressiveness or tightness of the table, but you should always consider these three fundamental factors first.

The rules for limit and no-limit hold'em are identical with the only difference between the two variations being the size of the bet allowed. However, it is these bet sizes that create two significant factors that affect all your strategic thinking. In limit hold'em:

1. More players stay in to see the flop. There is much less leverage exerted in limit games since the maximum bet is regulated, and as a result, many more players stay in to see the flop than in the no-limit variety. For example, in a no-limit game, it is not unusual for one player to raise and take the pot before the flop even occurs, and if the flop is seen, it is usually a heads-up pot. But in limit, with the cost to enter the pot being less, it is not unusual to see pots contested by five or more players. The lower cost of entry to see the flop means there is less bluffing and fewer chances for a big hand to narrow the field.

2. A showdown occurs much more often. With more hands in play, more players connect with the flop and a showdown often determines the winner of the hand. This means players need to play to the river with better hands, ones that can hold up when the cards are turned over.

These two major differences create a fundamentally different approach to strategic play and winning. You could sum it up like this: in no-limit, there is a greater emphasis on playing your opponents than on playing the cards, and in limit (particularly small stakes games), the opposite is true—there is a greater emphasis on playing the cards than on playing the opponents.

Let's begin at the beginning: your starting cards.

♦ STARTING CARDS AND THE FLOP ♦

The biggest mistake novices and habitually losing players make in hold'em is playing too many hands. Each call costs at least one bet, and if there is a raise, then two bets—or more. They compound this mistake when they catch a piece of the flop—but not enough of it—leading to more inadvisable bets and raises when they are holding a losing hand, thus making the situation even more costly. These lost chips add up quickly and set the stage for losing sessions.

So the foundation of playing winning hold'em is starting with solid cards, that is, playing the right cards in the right positions.

♦ THE TWO TYPES OF STARTING HANDS ♦

When considering whether to make a bet and enter the pot, you should think of your starting hand as being in one of two categories:

1. Big pairs that can win without improvement and big cards that can improve to pairs, two pairs, and three of a kind hands or better (which will beat smaller cards that likewise improve).

2. Small and medium pairs that will usually need a big improvement to win and draws, the draws that need to fill to straights and flushes, and the pairs that need to improve to a set.

1. Big Pairs and Big Cards

Limit hold'em is a game of big cards. Many pots will be determined at the showdown so you want to start with cards that are more likely to hold up after all the cards have been played out. Big cards tend to win more often than little cards when a showdown occurs. You'd rather have a pair of aces than a pair of eights at the river, and would choose two pairs of kings over sevens rather than two pairs of eights over sevens. Obviously, the bigger pairs are better in these confrontations because they'll win.

Big pairs and high cards play best against fewer opponents. With these hands, you usually want to narrow the field by raising so that fewer opponents can draw out on you with cards they would not have played in the first place if the cost was cheap.

So when you have big cards, you want to play against only a few opponents. And looking at it from the opposite viewpoint, if you are in a pot with just a few opponents, you generally only want to be in there with big cards.

2. Small and Medium Pairs, and Draws

Winning at limit hold'em is not only about holding big cards. Depending upon position and the action at the table, it can also be profitable to play smaller cards and more speculative hands as well, but only when the cost is cheap and you are up against multiple opponents. This category includes the **small pairs**, sevens or weaker, **medium pairs**, eights, nines, and tens, and **suited connectors**, consecutive cards such as 4-5 and 8-9 that are of the same suit.

When there are few players in the pot, the value in playing suited connectors drops and they become unprofitable to play. It is even worse if you call and try to play for one bet and then there is a raise behind you, because it will cost you even more money to play if you decide to call. In essence, you'll be chasing a small pot with a longshot hand that doesn't bring back enough value. However, you can play a raised pot with suited connectors when four or more players will see the flop, because you'll be getting the right odds to come in with this drawing hand.

Suited connectors need to connect with the flop for you to continue putting bets into the pot. Otherwise, you should probably fold them since their standalone strength is not promising. Of course, if you can see more cards for free, take them, but if you miss the flop, you've got an easy fold.

Similarly, if you can get in cheap, small and medium pairs can be seen to the flop, but if those three cards fall and you've got nothing, don't spend more chips. Think of it this way: "no set, no bet." Or "no three" (three of a kind), "let it be" (fold).

♦ SUITED CARDS ♦

Hands that are suited, such as J♦ 10♦ are always more valuable than a like hand that is unsuited, such as J♦ 10♠. The greater possibility of making a flush with suited cards adds value to hands. And though you'll only make a flush about 5% of the time when starting with two suited cards that get played to the river, the times you do connect can bring big pots. Your best flush, of course, is the **nut flush**, one led with an ace in your starting cards, but smaller flushes might win as well.

♦ FOUR CATEGORIES OF STARTING HANDS ♦

In this section, I outline a general starting approach to entering pots in limit and how the flop may affect these hands. But as always in hold'em and any brand of poker, you need to be flexible and mix up your play so that you don't get too predictable.

I've divided the starting hands into four different categories: Premium, Playable, Marginal, and Junk.

1. Premium Starting Hands

A-A   K-K   A-K   Q-Q   J-J

Aces, kings, queens, jacks, and A-K are the best starting hands. They are strong enough to raise from any position at the table and should be played aggressively. You hope to accomplish two things with the raise. First, you want to get more money into the pot on a hand in which you're probably leading, and second, you want to protect that hand by narrowing the field of opponents.

The greater the number of players who stay in the pot, the greater the chances that a weaker hand will draw out and beat your premium hand.

If a player raises ahead of you or reraises behind you, reraise with aces and kings, and just call with the other premium hands and see how the flop goes. Jacks are weaker than the other big pairs because there is about a 50% chance that an overcard, a queen, king, or ace will come on the flop, making your hand vulnerable.

If an overcard flops when you have jacks, queens, or even kings, or you miss entirely with A-K, you have to think about giving up on these hands if an opponent bets into you or check-raises. For example, if the flop is Q-7-6 and you have A-K or J-J, and an opponent leads into you, you're probably donating chips. A better flop would be K-10-3 for A-K or 10-8-2 for J-J.

It's also tough to play high pairs against an ace flop since players will often play starting cards containing an ace. And in low-limit games, you'll get players seeing the flop with all sorts of hands, so if there are a bunch of players in the pot, you have to be concerned about an ace flopping when you have a big pocket pair, such as queens or kings. If you have A-K, however, that ace-led flop puts you in a strong position, especially in a game where opponents like to play ace-anything.

You're also concerned with flops of three connecting cards, such as 8-9-10, and three suited cards if you don't have the ace of the same suit for a powerful nut flush draw. These are not good flops for big pairs or an A-K.

2. Playable Starting Hands

A-Q A-J A-10 K-Q 10-10 9-9 8-8

These starting hands should be folded in early position. They should also be folded in middle or late position if the pot has been raised from early position, which suggests strength, unless you think the raiser is loose and you can see the flop for just that one bet.

If players limp into the pot before you—that is, if they just call the bet—you can limp in as well with the Playable hands. Sometimes a raise will be good if you can force out players behind you and isolate the limper. However, if you're in there against loose players who are not easily moved off a pot, which will generally be the case in low limit, you might consider calling. When you're up against opponents who cannot be chased by raises, you'd prefer to see the flop for one bet with these hands.

If you enter the pot and it gets raised after you, you have to make a decision. If the raise comes from late position and it's from a loose player, you have more reason to call then to fold. It's just one bet. However, if it's raised twice and costs you two more bets, or it looks like you might be trapped between a bettor and a raiser, get away from these hands while it's still cheap. There is too much strength against you. The problem with A-Q, A-J, A-10, and K-Q in raised pots, is when you do connect. The ace-big hands could be outkicked by ace-bigger hands, leading to a lot of trouble. Always suspect opponents for premium cards, especially when they come into the pot from early position.

If you can get your pairs in to see the flop four-handed, you have enough value to handle a raise, but only if you're confident you won't be stuck between bettors and raisers while you're holding a less-than-premium hand.

What if no one has entered the pot before you? If you're in middle or late position, you should raise coming into the pot and try to limit the field or even better, get the blinds.

3. Marginal Starting Hands

7-7   6-6   5-5   4-4   3-3   2-2

K-J   K-10   Q-J   Q-10   J-10

A-x (ace with any other card)

Suited connectors: 5-6, 6-7, 7-8, 8-9, 9-10

Play marginal hands in early and middle position only if you can get in for one bet—but not at the cost of two bets. This means you'll fold these hands in raised pots or where you are vulnerable to being raised. The exception is with the small pairs (twos through sevens), where quantity equals quality. If you have reason to believe the pot will be played four-handed, you get the right odds to handle a raise, hoping to catch a set and win lots of chips.

In late position, call in an unraised pot, but if the pot has already been raised from early or middle position or you are between a bettor and a raiser, these marginal cards become unprofitable and should be folded.

If there is a raise after you enter the pot, you can call with these marginal hands—when the cost is only one bet—but fold in the face of a double raise or in situations where yet another raise can follow.

♠ Playing Late Position

You can play many more hands from late position. You've had a chance to see the betting before it's your turn to act. If the action is heavy, you fold all non-premium hands. If the action is light and the cost is cheap, you can get more creative. And if no one has entered the pot, you should often raise, as there is a good chance no one will call and you'll get the blinds.

If there are only limpers, you add suited connectors to your starting hands. Suited connectors are best played in a pot with three or more players. You want multiple opponents in the pot so that you can win a bunch of chips if you hit your hand. If the pot is raised and it would cost you two bets to play, call only if it looks like there will be enough players in to see the flop.

Pairs of twos through sevens are played similarly to connectors preflop. You want to play them in late position when you can see the flop cheaply and get a multiway pot. If there are several callers, you should call, but if the pot has been raised, meaning it will now cost you two bets to play, you can quietly muck the small pair. If you've already bet and the pot gets raised, you can call that extra bet as long as you feel that you won't get trapped and raised again.

Though a pair will only improve to a three of a kind hand about one time in eight, when it does, you'll be sitting with a big hand that can trap opponents for a lot of chips. If it doesn't improve and there are overcards on the flop, you probably have the worst of it and should fold against an opponent's bet. One rule of thumb here—no set, no bet.

4. Junk Hands

All other hands not shown in the above three categories should be folded. They are heavy underdogs with little chance of winning. If you're in the big blind and the pot is unraised, by all means take the flop for free. But if it costs you a full bet to see the flop, fold immediately. It's cheaper watching this round as a bystander.

♦ PLAYING THE BLINDS ♦

If you can get in the pot cheaply from the small blind, for just a few chips (you already have some chips in the pot), it is often worth expanding your starting cards to see if you catch a lucky flop. And if you're on the big blind and the pot is unraised, be careful never to fold—you get to see the flop for free!

♦ MORE ON THE FLOP AND AFTER ♦

If you miss the flop and think that betting will cause your opponent to fold, make the play. Otherwise, don't throw chips at longshots. Save them for better spots.

Be careful playing flush and straight draws unless they're to the **nuts**—the best hand possible given the cards on board. For example, you don't want to play a straight draw if there is a flush draw on board, or if you have, say the 6-7 on a board of 7-8-9-10-X. Any opponent with a jack will bust you here. And given that many players like to play J-10, that 7-8-9 flop is dangerous to your hand.

♠ Winning Bets and Saving Bets

If you think you've got the best hand, always bet or raise. Do not give opponents a cheap or free ride. You want to narrow the field and build the pot. If you have a huge hand, however, you want players to stay in the pot, but don't give away your hand by playing different than you usually would in the situation. If opponents expect you to bet, then bet.

Most important in limit hold'em and for that matter, all forms of poker, if you don't have the winning hand or a draw to a winning hand with enough money in the pot to go for, get out. Every bet you save in a lost pot is worth the same as a bet you'd win in a won pot. Minimize your bad bets and you'll most likely win money in this game.

♠ Further Discussion

For a more thorough discussion of flop, turn, and river play, look at the ideas discussed in the "thinking" subsections under flop, turn, and river play in the *No-Limit Hold'em Strategy* chapter (following) as they are similar, and for the most part, apply to all forms of hold'em. Also, further useful discussion in the same chapter is contained in the section, *15 Considerations on the Flop.*

11. NO-LIMIT HOLD'EM STRATEGY

In no-limit hold'em, your entire stack of chips is at risk on every single hand—as are those of your opponents. One big mistake and they're gone. Goodbye. In limit hold'em, one bet is only one bet. In no-limit, that one bet could be the defining moment of your game because it could be for all your chips. And that changes the way you play hands.

In no-limit, you must tread carefully every step of the way. What if you bet, say $25, on the preflop, and your opponent raises you all-in? Yikes! Now what do you do?

For a quick answer, you better have the goods, and I mean you *really* better have the goods if all your chips are on the line—or else you better fold your hand and give up the pot. Do you really want all your chips committed to an inferior hand (unless you're convinced your opponent doesn't hold that strong of a hand—big risk!) when you're barely getting your seat warmed?

Anyone can wave that big stick over another player and that changes the nature of every bet and move you make in no-limit. I call this type of intimidating big bet or the threat of one, the **hammer**. You must adjust for the possibility of an opponent

---

* The general strategy discussed in this chapter applies to both cash games and tournaments. Later, the *Tournament No-Limit Hold'em Strategy* chapter will focus on strategies that additionally and specifically apply to tournaments.

using the hammer and moving a massive number of chips into a pot against you. Or you might need to use the hammer against an opponent. And that requires fearlessness, the fortitude to put your chips on the line. It also requires that you know when your cards are better off folded, for a poor decision means that you'll lose all your chips—never a fun ending.

If you feel you've got guts to put all your chips on the line, then no-limit is the game for you.

♦ WHAT IS THE RIGHT AMOUNT TO BET AND RAISE IN NO-LIMIT? ♦

You find a hand you want to play, but now you wonder how much to bet. You look down at your stack. You can choose to risk anything from the minimum bet to all your chips. What to do?

Making a bet for the right amount is surprisingly easy—if you know what you're trying to accomplish.

Some players base the size of their bets on the strength of their hand. Mistake. Once opponents figures that out—and soon they will—it will be very easy for them to play against you and either blow you out of a pot where you have the better hand, or draw you deeper into a pot where they have the better hand.

Profitable poker is about deception. To achieve this in no-limit, you don't want to give your opponents any extra information. That means never showing them your cards unless they pay to see them at the showdown and never tipping them off by making bets that reflect the strength of your hand.

You achieve this deception by always betting or raising the same amount for the same type of situation. That way, when you bet, opponents are not wondering how strong your hand is but whether you *have* a hand. Big difference. You keep them off-balance, and that's exactly where you want them.

♣ PREFLOP STRATEGY

The blinds are posted, the cards are dealt, and the game has begun. You consider your options.

♦ BETTING ON THE PREFLOP ♦

If no player before you has entered the pot on the first round of betting, you have three choices: call the big blind, raise, or fold.

1. Calling

Of the three, calling is often the worst choice of all. Here's why:

A. If you come in weak (call) with *marginal* cards, a player after your position can raise and force you out.

Result: You've donated chips.

For example, you call with K-J from middle position, there are two callers and then a raise before it gets back to you. You're best off folding before tossing away any more chips.

B. If you come in weak (call) with *premium* cards, you allow opponents with marginal hands to see the flop and those hands might connect and improve to hands better than yours.

Result: You've allowed them to take your pot away, possibly at a big cost because you'll be defending those chips while you're second best.

For example, let's say you call with aces or kings and see the flop four-handed. You now have three opponents who can connect with the three cards in the middle. What happens if you bet the pot and are greeted by a huge raise? Maybe you have the best hand, maybe not. It may be a difficult call for you. Or, what happens if you just call and give opponents a free card? Now you're either really asking for trouble or getting no value out of a very premium pair.

There is a place for calling—when you want to see the flop cheaply with marginal cards, hoping to sneak in there and connect for a big hand, or when you want to slowplay pocket aces or kings for a big trap hand—but generally speaking, calling is the worst option of the three.

2. Raising

Raising makes opponents pay to play and lets you take the lead in betting, both of which are good things. It allows you to limit the field or eliminate it altogether, giving you the pot. If an opponent sees the flop with you, another bet will often eliminate him, or get him playing scared—unless he hits the flop big.

If you're the first player coming into the pot on the preflop, you generally want to enter the pot with a **standard raise**, three times the size of the big blind. If the big blind is at $5, make your raise $15, and if it's $10, make your raise $30. The reason you don't make the raise two times the big blind is that you make it too easy for your opponents, particularly the big blind, to enter the pot cheaply with marginal cards, subjecting your hand to lucky draws from opponents who might not otherwise see the flop.

A raise three times the size of the big blind is large enough to make it unprofitable for opponents to play marginal cards and junk. In other words, it takes away their favorable odds of seeing the flop (and possibly getting lucky)—something that would not be achieved with a raise two-times the size of the big blind (as in limit).

So, when no players have entered the pot, you want your preflop raises to consistently be three times the size of the big blind so that opponents get no extra information on the strength of your hand. Players that vary their preflop raises are sometimes announcing their hands.

And if one, two, or three of your opponents limp in to see the flop and you have a raising hand, make it four times the big blind. With more money in the pot, you want to make it unprofitable for the limpers to call your raise and continue playing. Plus, you would like to collect all their bets on the spot.

3. Folding

When your hand is not going to be profitable, it's best to fold. Calling with a weak hand has its virtues as discussed above, but can lead to losses if an aggressive player takes away the pot on the preflop or flop. You have this happen enough times and you begin to realize that the better play would have been to fold in the first place. If you can realize that before you donate chips to another players' cause, you will be that many chips to the richer.

♠ HOW MUCH TO RAISE PREFLOP ♠

• When you are the first player to enter the pot, raise three times the size of the big blind.

• If one, two, or three players limp into the pot, raise four times the size of the big blind.

♦ THINKING ON THE PREFLOP ♦

First things first: if you want to be a successful no-limit hold'em player, you can't play a lot of hands. In fact, most of the time, you'll fold hand after hand while you wait for either good hands or good situations before tossing chips down on the felt. No-limit hold'em is a game of patience, where the best strategy is to play few hands in the right positions and play them strong. This style of play is commonly called **tight-aggressive**; *tight* because you play few hands, and *aggressive*, because you bet and raise when you're in a pot, forcing opponents to play against a lot of pressure.

There are top players who can get away with playing very aggressively with a lot of hands because of superior people-reading skills. They pick up a lot of small pots by forcing opponents out with bets and raises. These players are not playing their cards but their opponents. As you get comfortable with the dynamics of no-limit hold'em, you can open up and play more hands in more situations. But as a newer player, playing a narrower range of hands—and playing them tough—will give you great opportunities to win money at cash games and tournaments.

The general guidelines in this section can help you decide when and how to enter the pot on the preflop in no-limit hold'em, what is often referred to as playing "A-B-C." They are the backbone of a solid strategy and give you a sense of the right play to make most of the time. However, if you make these plays *all* of the time, you'll be predictable and easier to read at the table. The circumstances of your situation—the tenor of the game, the types of players you are up against, and the dynamics of the table—will affect how often you'll deviate from these general guidelines. In a tournament, your chip count and that of your opponents, how deep in the tournament you are, and the pressure of the blinds and antes are all factors as well.

No-limit hold'em is a situational game. While the starting cards you hold are important, there are four other factors that determine the proper course to take when it is your turn to act.

For example, if you asked me how to play a pair of fives, my answer would be four questions:

1. What is your position at the table?
2. What kind of player is your opponent?
3. Did anyone bet before you?
4. Is the table tight or loose?

If you're playing in a tournament, I'd ask two more questions: how many chips do you have compared to the big blind? And how many does your opponents or opponent have compared to the big blind?

How you play fives is like asking what you do with a pistol when an adversary faces you. It depends; it always depends. If your adversary is a tank or an army, I suggest you back off. If your adversary holds a butter knife and you show the gun and a willingness to use it, I'd suggest your opponent would be the one to back down.

So what do you do when you have a pair of fives? *It depends.* As we go over the starting hands, we'll consider all the factors that will influence your decision on whether to commit chips to your starting hand, or fold the cards and wait for a better situation.

Meanwhile, what hands should you play? Let's begin with early position.

♦ EARLY POSITION ♦

The best starting cards in no-limit hold'em are the **premium hands**—pocket aces, kings, queens, jacks, A-K, and A-Q. In an unraised pot, bring these hands in for a standard raise in early position. Your goal is to either win the pot right there when all players fold or to narrow the field to one or two callers who will see the flop with you.

If you have aces or kings, hopefully you'll get a caller or two, or even better, a raiser. Then you'll raise or reraise the size of the pot or go in for all your chips if you get reraised. With queens and A-K, you can stand a raise to see the flop, but if the raise is for all your chips and you're not short-stacked, you may need to let these hands go. If you don't want your day finished with queens, you certainly don't want to go out on jacks or A-Q! If an opponent puts in a big raise or even goes all-in when you hold J-J or A-Q, these are grounds for folding these hands.

♠ ENTER STRONG EARLY, WEAK LATE ♠

The earlier your position, the stronger your cards need to be to enter the pot. The later your position, the weaker your cards can be.

If you have aces and kings and a player comes in raising before you, reraise, but if you've got a non-premium hand, fold. Lean towards calling with A-K and queens. If the raiser is tight, fold with A-Q and jacks; if the raiser is loose, raising or calling are both viable options. Remember, no play is set in stone in no-limit hold'em. Judge hands on a situation-by-situation basis.

Pass on all other hands from early position, especially against an aggressive table. If the table is tight or if it's early in a tournament and there's little cost to enter the pot, you can take a flier on a hand now and then to mix it up.

EARLY POSITION STARTING CARDS

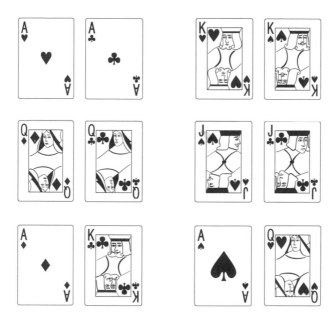

♦ MIDDLE POSITION ♦

In middle position, you can play more hands due to the simple fact that you have fewer players behind who can raise your bets. If there is a raise before your turn, consider folding all non-premium hands. You don't want to go into the flop as a big underdog, which this earlier position raise probably indicates. And if the raiser is tight, fold jacks and A-Q as well. If you have aces or kings, reraise and have no fear of getting all your chips in the middle. You can also reraise with queens and A-K, or you could just call.

If no one has raised in front of you, you will still play the premium hands for a raise and can add the second tier hands—eights, nines and tens, along with A-J, A-10, and K-Q—to your list of raising hands. If you get reraised by a player behind you, consider throwing second tier hands away. These hands have value, but against heavy betting, they're chip burners.

Of course, if your opponent is low on chips and moves in on the preflop, especially in a tournament, give him credit for holding lesser quality cards and be prepared to play all premium hands—but again, use judgment. When in doubt, go with your gut feeling.

What happens if a player behind you reraises? First, you have to look at who's raising. If you believe the player is on a bluff, consider calling. Also, if he's short-stacked and making a desperate play, you might play with him as well. The third reason to consider calling is if you think your opponent has read you for a steal and is on a resteal. You might also consider that the player feels you're weak and is trying to bully you. However, the majority of times, you have to give the raiser credit for holding strength. He is telling you that he's got better and you probably want to respect that and give up the pot. Weaker hands cannot stand a lot of heat.

You can also consider limping (calling and not raising) into the pot with the A-J, A-10, and the middle pairs, however, as a general rule, push at the pot and keep pressure on your opponents. Raising gives you the opportunity to win the pot right there while calling means you must continue fighting for it on the flop. If your raise is called, you'll know that your opponents fear the strength you've shown. You'll have more leverage after the flop with a good chance to get a free card or make a stab at the pot if they check into you, and lots to think about if they bet into you.

MIDDLE POSITION STARTING CARDS

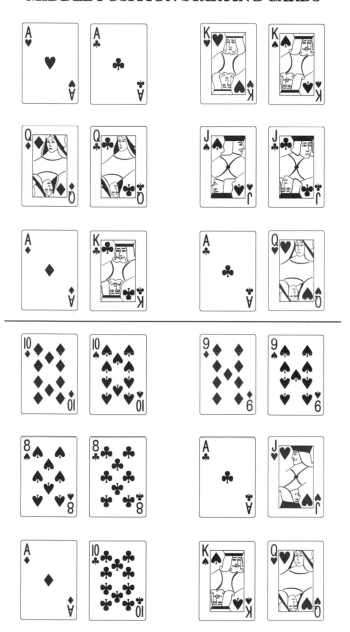

♦ LATE POSITION ♦

You'll play many more hands in late position than in early or middle position for the simple fact that you have few players after that who can raise your bets or reraise your raises and force you to fold. For example, if you are the player before the button, only the button and the two blinds can raise, and if you are on the button, you only have to worry about the two blinds. If the blinds play with you, they have the decided disadvantage of having to act before you on every round thereafter—that's three more betting rounds—the flop, turn, and river. That's a huge disadvantage to them. So when you're on the button or **cutoff seat** (the seat before the button), you have many more hands you can play safely and profitably.

This allows you to play hands you would not think about playing in middle position and certainly not in early position. If there have been raises prior to the action coming around to you, you can simply fold marginal hands without any cost at all, saving bets and chips. And that's why position is so important in hold'em.

If no one has raised the pot, you can expand your starting hands to any pair, an ace with any other card, and any two cards 10 or higher, Q-10 or K-J, for example. Generally, it's best to come in raising. Most of the time, you'll win the blinds, which is good. If you get callers, you have enough value to see the flop.

If you're in late position in an unraised pot, all pairs are playable. In addition to the premium pairs (jacks through aces) and the middle pairs (eights through tens), you should now play twos through sevens. If you can see the flop cheaply, you can also play suited connectors five or higher, such as 5-6, 6-7, 7-8, 8-9, and 10-J, hoping to make two pair, trips, straight or flush draws, or best of all, a made straight or flush.

If you get aces or kings in late position and you think you'll get a caller, raise. If not, it might be better to limp in. You don't get kings or aces often, but when you do, you want to make money on them.

When you're playing in steal positions—and late positions are steal positions—opponents will not give you as much credit for a good hand because they're figuring you to steal the pot, which of course, sometimes you will be doing, And you should give them less credit for strong hands as well. So when you catch good on the preflop, you are in great position to not only steal the blinds, but trap opponents who try to resteal on you or give you action because you're playing position.

If the situation is right for a steal, meaning you have players behind you who won't defend their blinds, any two cards are valid raising hands: J-8, 9-7, 3-2—even 7-2, the worst starting hand in hold'em.

♠ Playing Premium Hands in Late Position

If you're in late position and the pot has been raised by a player in early position, reraise with A-A, K-K, Q-Q, and A-K. If you get reraised, you may consider just calling with Q-Q and A-K, and if the raiser is tight and goes all-in, you probably want to release these hands. You certainly do not want to be in that reraised pot with jacks, A-Q, or anything less. But with aces and kings, you're always ready to play for all the marbles preflop.

If the pot is raised by a player in middle position, reraise with the top four hands, A-A, K-K, Q-Q, and A-K. How you play jacks and A-Q is a judgment call, but it may be safer just to call and see the flop.

♦ PLAYING THE BLINDS ♦

The blinds have the advantage of going last in the first round of play but the big disadvantage of going first in all other rounds. Sometimes you get lucky as the big blind and get either

LATE POSITION STARTING CARDS

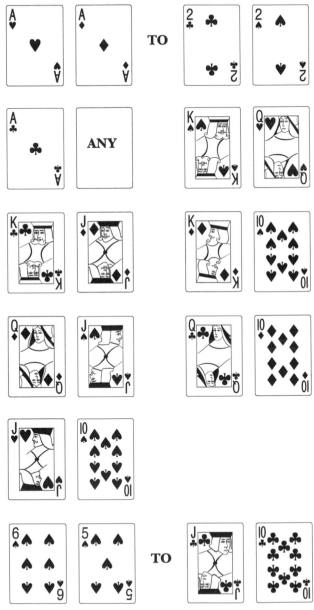

(Suited Connectors)

a free ride because no player has raised, or a free pot because all players have folded.

Playing the blinds is easy. If you're in the small blind and everyone folds to you or there are only callers and you can see the flop cheaply, it's not a bad play to call the big blind. You may flop something pretty or check to the showdown and win with better garbage than your opponent. If the cost is cheap to see three more cards, the profit potential is enormous if you catch a big hidden hand and get played with by an opponent. So throwing away a few chips here and there is not costly when you consider the big windfall you may get if you flop a monster.

If there is no raise and you're in the big blind with a hand you don't want to raise with, always see the flop for free. Don't make the mistake of folding!

If there's a raise from early or middle position, fold anything but premium hands. You're asking for trouble to bump up against players showing strength, especially when you'll have to act before them on the next three betting rounds. If there is a raise from late position, suspect the player for a steal, especially if this opponent is making a habit of it. You'll need to start defending your blinds if they're constantly being stolen, so pick a good spot to raise right back when you think your opponent can be forced out of the pot. You can raise, of course, with all premium hands, as well as hands you normally wouldn't play from early position but which do have some strength: ace-anything, K-Q, K-J, or any two high cards.

You are out of position in the blinds, meaning you will have to play first on every other betting round if you decide to enter the pot. You're vulnerable to raises behind you, so you need strength to play from the blinds. Keep in mind that you're in early position, so play your hands according to the advice in the early position strategy section.

♦ OTHER STARTING HANDS: ALL POSITIONS ♦

♠ Ace-Something Starting Hands

Many new players get overly excited about hands containing an ace, particularly suited aces that have flush possibilities. However, ace-something hands smaller than A-K can spell a lot of trouble for you. With A-K, you hope to flop an ace or a king, either of which will give you top pair, top kicker. Unless your opponent has flopped a monster, you most likely have the best hand and can play it aggressively.

For example, if two suited cards come on board, you'll want to put a big bet into the pot to protect your top pair-top kicker hand and chase opponents out of the pot. Your big bet takes away the correct odds for a player going for a flush or straight.

Making top pair-top kicker on the flop means you flopped really good and that is the value of A-K hands when they connect. Problematic hands occur when you have less than a king as a kicker and then get your ace, or if you start with two high cards and connect with one of them such that you don't have top pair-top kicker. These types of hands are called **trouble hands**, because you could be playing a hand that actually connects with the flop, but is outkicked or outpaired and subject to losing lots of chips. So hands such as A-Q, A-J, K-Q—really ace-anything or king-anything—have to be played carefully if there is aggressive betting.

♠ Playing Trash Hands

One great way to mix up your play and stay unpredictable is to come into the pot raising with trash hands—starting cards that normally wouldn't be strong enough to play. You have three goals when you're playing with the garbage.

1. Steal the blinds and antes.

2. If you get a caller and get a lucky flop, you can really break an opponent. For example, if you enter the pot with 8-5 and the flop comes 4-6-7 or A-8-5, you've got a hand that is impossible for your opponent to put you on. And if his starting cards were A-K on the A-8-5 flop, he's way behind and set up to lose a bunch of chips.

3. If you come at the flop aggressive, you may be able to push your opponent off the pot with your double bluff regardless of what falls.

However, keep in mind that trash hands are trash hands because, in the long run, they're big underdogs to win if the betting goes to a showdown. So don't make a habit of playing trash. But now and then to mix things, up, playing trash against the right opponents in the right situations can pay dividends.

◆ BEWARE TELEVISED POKER ◆

Many new players, excited by the world class poker they see on television, emulate the hands they see the pros playing at the final table. They'll wonder why I don't advocate playing those hands here. The answer is simple. Final table television poker is not a realistic reflection of how no-limit hold'em is played and if you follow what you learn by watching television, you're going to get destroyed at the game. There are four major reasons for this:

1. Very few hands are shown on television leading viewers to believe that the cards shown are the ones typically played in a regular game. The fact is, they're not. The broadcasts don't show the many, many hands that are tossed away by players.

2. You're not getting a sense of tournament dynamics, where a player is often forced to make moves to protect a short stack, while another bets on cards to mix up his game. Other times, he may spot an opportunity that is not about the cards, but the situation.

3. You're often watching short-handed tables or heads-up action, where the hands that are correct to play are entirely different from tables with a full complement of eight or more players.

4. A trash hand may be featured because the play of it was interesting or the pot was large. For every hand shown, there may be hundreds that were played and not shown, with the hands actually televised not being at all representative of typical ones played.

♣ FLOP STRATEGY

You're in to see the flop with one or more opponents. You watch the dealer turn over the three cards, and you have to make some decisions. It's your turn to play...

♦ BETTING ON THE FLOP ♦

If you are first to act on the flop or the betting has been checked to you, you have three choices: check, fold, or bet. Much of what was covered in the preflop section above applies here. Taking the lead and pushing players gives you a better chance of winning the pot than playing passive. If you bet, your opponents may fold; you win. If you don't bet, they won't fold—but you might if one of them takes the lead instead.

When you are the first to bet after the flop, a pot-sized bet is standard. So if $35 is in the pot, bet around $35. If you're in a tournament with a pot sitting at $3,000, push $3,000 out there. Pot-sized bets make it expensive for marginal hands to call and give hands of decent strength reason enough to reconsider the price of entry. You can sometimes have the same effect by **underbetting** the pot—making a bet that is one-third smaller than the size of the pot or less—but the best play is usually to go with pot-sized bets.

Overbetting the pot—making a bet that is greater than about one and one-half the size of the pot (for example, betting around $150 when the pot has about $100)—or going all-in, really puts opponents to the test. When you overbet, you're looking to get opponents to fold, or sometimes to trap them into calling when you have a great hand and they suspect you for a bluff.

♠ HOW MUCH TO BET ON THE FLOP ♠

• When you are the first player to enter the pot, raise about the size of the pot.

• Underbetting the flop or overbetting the flop are plays that can be effective as well.

♦ THINKING ON THE FLOP ♦

When the flop hits the board, the real play in hold'em begins. Unless you have the **nuts**, the absolute best hand possible given the cards on board, nothing is for sure when the flop hits the table. You might flop great, but an opponent might have flopped better. But most of the time, you'll flop nothing, with your opponents in the same predicament.

So who gets the pot when neither player makes a powerful hand?

In no-limit, it is the player who goes out and gets it. Betting, raising, and putting pressure on opponents causes them to fold. The great players keep pushing their opponents with bets and raises and take the pot right there or on the next betting round with continued aggressive play. If that doesn't work, they're able to read their opponents for strong hands and fold before they lose too many chips and get hurt. So we're back to the two themes of what makes a successful poker player: *aggression* and *reading opponents*.

If you came in raising preflop, you want to continue playing aggressively. If you're first, bet regardless of what flops. Your opponent will probably fold and you've got the pot. If he calls and you don't improve, you might consider checking on the turn. If he raises you, it's a tough call, but you'll have to consider giving up the hand unless you feel you've got better. Now, if you're second, and he checks, bet out at him.

What if he bets into you? If you miss the flop, give him the pot. Since you've shown strength preflop, his bet on the flop means you're probably second-best.

When you have what you think is the best hand, your goal is to take the pot immediately, particularly when there are straight and flush draws possible, for example, two cards of the same suit are on the board. You don't want opponents playing for another card cheaply, making it, and then destroying you on a hand that shouldn't have even seen another card. If opponents are going to beat you, make them pay to do so.

However, if you have an absolute monster like a full house or quads, you want to keep players in and extract more bets out of them. Often, that means checking and hoping a free card gives them a bigger hand.

It's not always easy to tell where you stand when the flop hits. You could be better, worse, or about even with your opponents. Poker players get their clues from how their opponents bet and react to bets. We'll look at a few situations to see how this might work.

Let's say you start out with a pair of sevens and the flop comes 7-J-Q, all in spades. This is a great flop for you—a set!—except for one problem. Those three spades make a flush possible. You bet, an opponent raises to $50, you reraise to $150, and he pushes all his chips in the middle! Now what do you do? You've got a big decision to make. You've got a powerful hand, a set of sevens, but if it's not the best hand, you lose all your chips—on one hand!

Or maybe you start out with big slick, A-K, and *almost* get a great flop: A-J-10 of mixed suits. You've got top pair, the aces, and top kicker. Normally you're feeling pretty good in this situation, except that your raise is met with an all-in reraise. If your opponent is holding K-Q, he's flopped a straight, and given his strong betting, you have to suspect that possibility. Of course, he could have J-10 for two pair, or A-J for a stronger two pair. Perhaps he has that same A-K. Players tend to play big cards in hold'em and all these scenarios are possible given his aggressive stance. He might even have pocket tens or jacks and be holding a set.

Maybe he's bluffing. And maybe he's not.

So what do you do? It depends, it *always* depends. *What does he have?* Well, that's going to cost all your chips to find out.

Now you're playing poker. If your opponent is tight, you have to give serious consideration to giving up this pot, and if he is a maniac, betting and raising wildly, you have to consider the opposite. On the surface, given the strong betting on this ace-high flop with all the possibilities we just discussed, he has to figure you for at *least* aces, so when he's coming back with an all-in raise, you have to figure him for something stronger. Folding your hand may be the best play, but you have to evaluate the situation to make the best decision.

There are few situations in no-limit where the answer is

always the same no matter what is going on. The key to making the best decision is understanding how your opponent plays and what he might have. "But," you might say, "how can I do that if I can't see his cards." Well, you may not be able to see his cards, but you can see how he is betting, and how he is reacting to betting, and from what position at the table he is doing all this. You also have to consider how he views your play.

Sometimes you can get clues from how he reacts to situations physically. It's like a detective solving a case. He's working with incomplete information because he didn't witness the crime, just like you have incomplete information because you can't see your opponent's cards. The detective can examine all sorts of information, sifting through the facts, weighing evidence and motives, until he has a pretty good clue as to what happened. In poker, you're faced with a similar situation. You're given a bunch of clues, now you have to piece them together. By paying close attention to how an opponent plays, you can get a pretty good idea of where you stand in a hand.

You'll be wrong sometimes and will be bluffed out of pots where you have the best hand or suckered into pots where your opponents have the best hand. But again that's poker. You won't always be right. However, the more you study the game and the more you play, the more accurate you will get at reading opponents.

♠ Fifteen Considerations on the Flop

1. If you miss the flop and an opponent bets into you, strongly consider folding. For example, if you start with A-K and the flop comes J-8-7, you've got nothing. Maybe your opponent is bluffing, but so what? You can't win every hand. And maybe he's not bluffing. Either way, you don't have much.

2. Say you start with a medium or small pocket pair

and don't catch a third card to form a three of a kind. Bet if you think you can take the pot and check if you don't think you can. In other words: no set, no bet. You've missed the flop. Be careful about investing more chips into it.

3. If you start with a medium or small pocket pair and *catch* a third card to form a set, you're sitting pretty and want to extract as many chips as possible out of your opponents. That might mean either betting because they expect you to bet, checking to let them catch up with another card on the turn, or letting them take the lead if they're aggressive.

4. Trouble hands part A: Hands like A-Q, A-J, and A-10 are called trouble hands because if an ace flops, they're vulnerable to aces with bigger kickers. If you see a flop such as A-J-5 when you have A-Q and your opponent holds A-K, you can get hurt pretty bad. You would rather see the queen, your kicker, connecting. A flop of Q-10-3 is much better for the A-Q because you now have top pair and top kicker.

5. Trouble hands part B: Hands like K-Q and K-J are called trouble hands because if a king flops, your hand is vulnerable to the A-K. In a raised pot, be careful because that raise indicates preflop strength, which may be trouble for you.

6. Pocket kings are the second best hand you can start with, but if an ace flops, you can get into deep trouble if an opponent holds a pocket ace. In 2005, a player at my table busted out of the World Series of Poker after less than 45 minutes of play because he played his kings for an all-in bet after an ace flopped. He was shocked when he lost the hand and all his chips, but nobody else at the table was.

7. Similarly, pocket queens lose their luster if an ace or king flops, especially given that players are more likely to play high cards. Pocket queens want to see flops such as J-8-6, where there are no overcards to the queen.

8. If you're drawing to a straight, you have to be concerned about two suited cards on the flop and *very* concerned if there are three suited cards on the board. Always be aware of flush possibilities when you're drawing to a straight.

9. If you start with a big pocket pair, you're probably still ahead on the flop as long as there are no overcards, no pair on board (possible three of a kind, full house, or quads), and no straight or flush draws. Make opponents put chips into the middle if they want to play with you.

10. Say you flop a set but are worried that an opponent flopped a bigger set. For example, you start out with fours and the flop is J-7-4. The simple strategy here is to play your set of fours like it is the boss. Set over set is possible but you can't play scared. The same goes for the preflop when you get into a betting war holding kings and are worried about your opponent having pocket rockets. As poker players say, "You can't get away from that hand."

11. When you've got the lead and the flop comes with cards that give opponents straight or flush draws, bet heavy and make them pay the price to go for their draws. For example, if you have A♦ K♥ and the flop is K♠ 10♠ 6♥, you've got top pair top kicker but one more spade gives an opponent a possible flush. Make a pot-sized bet and make it unprofitable for an opponent to call. If you don't take the pot there, you'll be letting him play cheaply. If another spade falls and an opponent bets big, he either takes you out of the pot (and maybe he's bluffing!) or you'll play with him. Win or lose, you shouldn't have allowed him to play.

12. You flop top pair-top kicker. For example, you have A-K and see a flop like A-10-3 or K-J-4. Bet and make opponents pay to play, you're probably leading. If they fold, take the pot—it's yours. However, be careful if an opponent plays back at you for a lot of chips. Suspect a big hand or big draw.

13. You have an overpair to the flop. Let's say you start with pocket nines and the flop comes 8-5-2. Bet and make opponents pay to see more cards or allow them to give you the chips in the middle.

14. You have an underpair to the flop; say a pair of fours. The flop comes J-8-6. You don't necessarily have the worst hand against an opponent who is playing aggressive and pushing you around. It's a tough call to make if he bets into you, but sometimes your instincts will tell you to play against some bets. If you read your opponent for a hand such as an A-K or A-Q, you've got the better hand. These kinds of situations occur all the time in no-limit hold'em.

15. You don't always have to bet the flop. Change up your play sometimes. Don't be predictable. Also, a free card is not always a bad thing.

♣ TURN STRATEGY

You're further into the hand now. You've played your starting cards through the preflop and flop and now watch as a fourth card hits the board. It's your turn to play…

♦ BETTING ON THE TURN ♦

If you're first to bet, you have four choices: check, underbet the pot, make a pot-sized bet, or overbet the pot. You have to ask yourself whether you want your opponent to put more chips into the pot or fold and give the pot to you? You encourage him to fold, of course, by putting chips into the pot (betting). Underbetting means an opponent has to pay to play with you and gets chips in the middle. Making a pot-sized bet usually induces an opponent to fold, and you give him extra encouragement by putting even more chips into the pot.

The more chips you bet, the more reason an opponent has to fold, but at the same time, the more risk you take if he doesn't fold and has the better hand. Overbetting the pot as a way to get an opponent to fold risks more chips than you need to get the job done and is generally not the best idea on the turn.

If you think a bet will get an opponent to lay down stronger cards, make that bet. If you think you've got the best hand, try to get more chips into the pot. You don't want to give opponents a chance to improve for free.

Betting smaller than one-third less than the size of the pot (underbetting) or betting about the full size of the pot (pot-sized bet) are generally the most effective sized bets on the turn.

♠ HOW MUCH TO BET ON THE TURN ♠

If you've got the best hand, think you can get the better hand to lay down the cards, or want more chips in the pot, the most effective bets on the turn are usually at least one third less than the size of the pot up to the full size of the pot, depending on the situation.

♦ THINKING ON THE TURN ♦

The turn is a betting round that will test your people-reading skills. How will your opponents react to a bet or check if you go first, and how will you react if they go first?

If you've played aggressively on the preflop and flop and your opponent hasn't budged, you have to figure him for possible strength. It's time for you to look at what you think *he* *thinks* you have. If you're representing strength and playing tight, you have to give him credit for a strong hand and slow down your betting unless you're confident that you've got a better hand. If he checks, you check, and if you're first, check to him and see how he reacts.

The turn is a time to put the brakes on a bluff that didn't work and possibly ease your way into the river with a hand that can't weather much more betting. If your opponent is weak, he may check along with you. This may be a clue that you can zap him out on the river or play it slow and see who shows down better. You can always push your bluff one more bet, but if your opponent saw you through on the flop, this could be dangerous.

You've felt your opponents out on the flop. How they played on the flop greatly influences the types of hands you think they may be playing. Use your best judgments and go with them. If you think a bet may push a weak opponent out of the pot, betting is a strong option. If you're not sure, checking is not a bad option. And if you think you have the best hand, get more chips into the pot.

♣ RIVER STRATEGY

The last card hits the board, making it five cards that you'll share with your opponents. The pot is either going to be yours or it will belong to an opponent. It may depend on how the betting goes...

♦ BETTING ON THE RIVER ♦

When you have a big hand that you're confident is the best, you want to get more chips into the pot. Sometimes this means underbetting the pot, sometimes it means making a pot-sized bet, and sometimes it means going all-in. You have to know your opponent to make the best play. If you're last and there have been no bets, put the amount of chips in the pot you feel your opponent will call. If you're first, you have two options: check or bet. If your opponent is very aggressive or has been leading at the pot, you can consider checking and letting him bet, then going over the top of him with a raise to try and get more chips in the pot.

You want to be careful not to move an opponent off a pot with a bet, but at the same time, you want to get more chips into the pot. Checking risks "losing" chips you could have induced into the middle. Often, making an underbet is a good way to get more chips out of your opponent. You make it tempting enough so that he feels he has to call. However, your knowledge of how your opponent plays should guide you.

When you're bluffing, going with a pot-sized bet or an oversized or all-in bet can put enough chips on the table to force out an opponent. Beginners sometimes make the mistake of bluffing too timidly on the river, tossing in too few chips relative to the pot size. If you're going to bluff at the river, make sure it's for enough chips that your opponent will be faced with a difficult decision on whether to call.

The worst thing you can do on the river is attempt to bluff out a player who is holding a monster hand! We all have our stories of trying to bluff out nut flushes and full houses—somehow, they don't move off the pots so easily. It happens sometimes, but if you pay careful attention, you'll mostly avoid this unpleasant surprise.

♠ HOW MUCH TO BET ON THE RIVER ♠

• If you're not sure that you have the best hand, strongly consider checking. If you bet and a raise will drive you from the pot, making that first bet may be a mistake.

• If you do have the best hand, bet the amount that will get you a call.

• Bluffing with any sized bet—underbetting the pot to making an all-in bet—can be a big play here but proceed carefully. Don't take foolish risks.

♦ THINKING ON THE RIVER ♦

When you have a strong hand but have doubts about whether it's the best one out there, it's often better to check at the river, rather than bet. Here's why:

1. You'll usually get called by a player who is holding a better hand! This loses both the pot *and* your river bet.

2. If an opponent raises you, you'll probably have to fold and lose the pot and your river bet.

3. If your opponent has a worse hand, he'll usually fold. So you get no extra chips.

In the first two instances, you've lost not just the pot, but your river bet as well. Minimizing lost chips is essential to winning at poker. In the third instance, you haven't lost chips, but you've risked chips to win a hand you would have won anyway.

If you check with a hand of moderate strength and your opponent checks, you'll see the showdown with no further cost. If he bets, you see what you want to do.

You should bet first on the river only when you feel reasonably confident that you can get an opponent with a better hand to fold, or when you want to get more chips into the pot because you feel you have a better hand.

If an opponent checks to you, and you have the best hand, bet so that you get value for the cards—but only if you're confident that your opponent doesn't have you pegged as an aggressive player that he can trap with a check-raise. Bluffing is always an option—but again, it must be for enough chips to be effective—as is checking to see the showdown.

♦ MORE ON CASH GAMES ♦

In cash games, you're not worried about blinds, because they're generally small, nor are you concerned with antes, because there aren't any. Your goal in a cash game is purely and simply to win chips. You don't care if you have more chips than other players, or less, as long as you finish with more of them than you started with. And then you have won money.

When you have a good session and win lots of chips, you can take them off the table and leave any time you want. The chips you play with can be converted to real profits whenever you choose.

12. TOURNAMENT BASICS

Tournaments are a blast. They not only offer you a chance to compete for thousands of dollars in prize money in small-buy-in tournaments, but for tens of thousands, hundreds of thousands, and yes, millions of dollars in large buy-in tournaments such as you see at the World Series of Poker or on the World Poker Tour.

And forgetting the money for a few seconds—and *only* for a few seconds—the competition and fun of tournament poker, especially no-limit games, is simply lots of fun, worth every penny of your entry fee.

So what does it take to enter a poker tournament? Only money. That's it. Unlike professional baseball, basketball, golf, or any other sport where you have to earn your way onto the professional circuit, the world of poker is purely egalitarian. Put up your money and you can play.

Whether played online or in a land-based casino, tournaments work pretty much according to the same principles. Even the biggest tournaments are open to all players who want to participate and are very simple to enter: just show up and hand over your entrance fee!

And how about WPT events and the World Championships? Ditto. Put up the loot and get on your playing suit. You may be the lucky soul that goes all the way, as did Chris Moneymaker in 2003, when he won the World Championship and $2.5 million,

Greg Raymer in 2004 when he cashed in for $5 million, or Joseph Hachem in 2005 when his first-place finish was worth $7.5 million.

Dream on, my friend, you could be next!

◆ OVERVIEW ◆

A **tournament** is a competition in which players start with an equal number of chips and play until one player holds all of them. It is a process of elimination, a gladiator contest where the last player remaining will be the winner. As players lose their chips and are eliminated from play, the remaining competitors get consolidated into fewer tables. What might start out as a 120-player event played at a dozen ten-handed tables will get reduced to eleven tables, and then ten tables, and so on, as players bust out.

Eventually, the field will be narrowed down to just one table, the **final table**, where the prestige and big money is earned. And that table will play down until just one player is left holding all the chips—the **champion**. Your goal is to be that last player so you can win the big prize, or at the very least, to finish **in the money**, that is, win a cash prize by finishing among the top players.

In big events, winners can take home in excess of one million dollars. The main event in the 2005 World Series of Poker awarded over $1 million dollars each to every one of the final table contestants! In fact the total prize pool of over $50 million in the final event alone made it the biggest money sporting event in the world!

◆ TOURNAMENT BUY-INS ◆

Here is how a tournament works. Every player buys in for a set amount of money. It could be any amount, $20, $30,

$50, $100, $120, $500, or $1,000—really, any amount that the tournament organizer decides to set. Local events are moderately priced, with affordable entry fees that keep the tournaments filled with players. These events are usually under $100 to enter. The big tournaments, such as the main event in the World Series of Poker (WSOP) and on the World Poker Tour (WPT), have buy-ins of $10,000 or even $25,000! The high stakes players and professionals love these events because the prize pools are worth millions of dollars, with the winner usually receiving in excess of $1 million. That's a lot of money!

♦ REBUY AND FREEZE-OUT TOURNAMENTS ♦

There are two types of tournaments—freeze-outs and rebuy tournaments. A **freeze-out tournament** is a do or die structure. Once you run out of chips, you are eliminated. Unlike a cash game, you can't go back into your pocket for more chips.

In a **rebuy tournament**, you can purchase additional chips which is usually allowed only when your chip stack is equal to or less than the original starting amount and only during the first few specified rounds of play. This is called the **rebuy period**. Some tournaments allow limited rebuys, and others allow players to rebuy as often as they go broke, that is, until the rebuy period is over.

At the end of the rebuy period, most tournaments allow you to get an **add-on** as well—a final purchase of a specific amount of additional chips. Usually, only one add-on is permitted per player, though some events allow double add-ons, and rarely, even more.

Once the rebuy period is over, you're playing in pure survival mode. If you lose your chips, you are eliminated and your tournament is over.

Tournaments with entry fees under $100 are usually played

as rebuy tournaments, while those with buy-ins greater than $1,000 are typically freeze-outs. The bigger money events like the ones you see on television featuring the top pros are almost always freeze-out tournaments.

♠ TOURNAMENTS COMPARED TO CASH GAMES ♠

Five differences between tournaments and cash games:

1. Starting chip counts. In tournaments, all players start with the same number of chips. In cash games, players may start with as many chips as they want to buy within any minimum or maximum amounts that may be set by the cardroom.

2. Getting more chips. Unless the tournament is a rebuy or add-on event, once you lose your chips, you are eliminated. That is it. In rebuy and add-on events, players can only rebuy or add-on during the first three levels or so. After that period is over, there is no coming back once you're eliminated. In cash games, you can always buy in for more.

3. Cash value of chips. Tournament chips are worthless at face value. They are only good within the tournament as a means of survival and power. Chips used in cash games are worth exactly the chip amount printed on the chip.

4. Start and finish time. Tournaments have a set starting time and end when you lose your chips, with the tournament itself ending when one player holds all the chips. In cash games, you can start and quit any time you want.

5. Possible wins. In bigger tournaments, the prize pools offer players a shot at huge lottery-sized winnings that, for the average player, would not normally be possible to win in a lifetime's worth of play. In cash games, the winning potential is mostly determined by the limits played.

♦ SATELLITES AND SUPER SATELLITES ♦

In the 1970s, the Horseshoe Casino in Las Vegas came up with a great concept to increase attendance in the main event of the World Series of Poker. It was pretty clear that few players could afford or were willing to cough up $10,000 entry fees. But if they could get in for less...

And so they came up with a great concept: **satellites**. For a fraction of the cost of the main event, players could enter a one-table mini-tournament of ten players, where the winner would earn a seat into the main event. If a player put up $1,000 and beat the other nine players at his table, he'd have a $10,000 entry and a chance at the big prize. And that is exactly what happened to Tom McEvoy when he parlayed a satellite win into the World Championship in 1983.

Eventually, the satellite concept was expanded to include multiple-table tournaments that awarded entries to multiple winners. These events, called **super satellites**, have become enormously popular. The supers attract hundreds of players and can award dozens of seats to the top finishers. The World Series of Poker traditionally offers $225 buy-in super satellite tournaments with one seat awarded to every 40 players. For the top finishers in these supers, it's a really inexpensive way to have a shot at millions. Other tournaments also may have relatively inexpensive super satellite entry fees for their main $10,000 or higher events or they may make the entry fees $1,000. This allows many more players to win their entry (with one seat awarded to every ten entrants).

And it is not just the host casinos that offer these events just prior to their tournaments, but the online poker rooms as well. Online casinos send thousands of satellite and super satellite winners to the World Series of Poker every year. Interestingly, online sites supply more players to the WSOP than any other source. That's how World Champion Chris Moneymaker got there in 2003. Moneymaker was able to parlay a $39 entry fee for an online tournament into a championship and $2.5 million! And in 2004, Greg Raymer, following in Moneymaker's footsteps, turned an online entry into $5 million. Second place finisher David Williams, who also qualified online, earned $2.5 million!

The possibility of playing on poker's biggest stage for a fraction of the $10,000 cost has helped fuel the enormous growth in poker.

For all major WSOP and WPT events, satellites and super satellites are available, days, weeks, or even many months in advance, either at the host casino or at online poker rooms,. Local poker clubs also run tournaments, so if you want to try your hand at a major event, keep your eyes open and you'll find lots of opportunities to earn your way.

♦ TOURNAMENT STRUCTURE ♦

Tournaments are divided into **levels** or **rounds**. Each level is marked by an increase in the amount of chips players are forced to commit to the pot before the cards are dealt. The blinds slowly increase, and after a few levels, the antes kick in. Levels may be as short as fifteen or twenty minutes in low buy-in events that are designed to be completed in as little as a few hours, or as long as ninety minutes to two hours for major events that are structured to last up to a week.

Typically, every ninety minutes or two hours in a tournament, you will be given a ten or fifteen minute break.

Each event is set up differently by the tournament director and the length of the rounds and structure for increasing the blinds and antes will be posted in advance on a board or printed on sheets you can pick up in the playing area, usually by the registration desk.

In general, the greater the amount of money at stake, the longer the tournament. Short, quick rounds such as those used in low-limit events, make for faster play and introduce a greater element of luck as you're forced to play more aggressively to stay ahead of the quickly increasing blinds and antes. In the bigger events, you're given more chips to start, the levels are longer, and the increase in blinds and antes is more gradual so that you can get a lot more play. This combination lends itself to the skill factor playing a larger role in tournaments with longer and more gradual levels than is the case at the more hurried low-limit tournaments.

The speed of a tournament is regulated by the blind and ante structures. When the forced bets are low, there is no real pressure for players to play hands. They can sit and wait for premium hands and optimal situations. On the other hand, as you go deeper into a tournament, the blinds and antes get more expensive, and the price of sitting passively and not playing hands is high. If your stack isn't large enough, as few stacks are, you will get blinded and anted out if you don't make some plays.

Of course, in any tournament, no matter how big or how small—or any cash game as well—the element of luck is always a factor. However, the greater your level of skill and the better you play, the more chances you have of getting into the money or winning the tournament. Yes, there is luck, but never downplay the amount of skill involved in succeeding in tournament poker. Once you play your first event, this will be eminently clear. And the more you play, the more you'll see how your decision-making creates your own destiny and affects your chances of winning the whole pie.

Sometimes the turn of a card can make or break you in an event, but the events leading up to the decisive moment, the number of chips you gained or lost, and the decisions you made, all have a part.

Following, is a fairly typical payout schedule. You'll notice that the first three rounds have only blind bets, and it isn't until the fourth round that antes kick in as well.

LEVELS/ANTES/BLINDS CHART #1

This sample structure gives each player $1,000 or $2,000 in starting chips.

Level	Ante	Blinds
1	-	25-50
2	-	50-100
3	-	100-200
4	25	100-200
5	25	200-400
6	50	300-600
7	75	400-800
8	100	600-1,200
9	200	800-1,600
10	300	1,000-2,000
11	500	1,500-3,000
12	1000	2,000-4,000
13	1000	4,000-8,000
14	2000	5,000-10,000

LEVELS/ANTES/BLINDS CHART #2

This sample structure gives each player $500 in starting chips.

Level	Ante	Blinds
1	-	25-25
2	-	25-50
3	-	50-100
4	-	100-200
5	25	100-200
6	50	150-300
7	75	200-400
8	100	300-600
9	200	500-1000
10	200	800-1600
11	300	1000-2000

Raise limits after this every 20 minutes, maybe to this

12	500	1500-3000
13	1000	2000-4000
14	1000	4000-8000

LEVELS/ANTES/BLINDS CHART #3

Here's a sample structure with $10,000 in starting chips.

Level	Ante	Blinds
1	-	50-100
2	-	100-200
3	25	100-200
4	25	150-300
5	50	200-400
6	75	300-600
Race off $25 chips		
7	100	400-800
8	100	600-1,200
9	200	800-1,600
10	300	1,000-2,000
11	400	1,500-3,000
12	500	2,000-4,000
13	500	3,000-6,000
Race off $100 chips		
14	1000	4,000-8,000
15	1000	6,000-12,000
16	2000	8,000-16,000
17	3000	10,000-20,000
18	4000	15,000-30,000
Race off $500 chips		
19	5000	20,000-40,000
20	5000	30,000-60,000
21	10000	40,000-80,000
22	10000	60,000-120,000

♦ STARTING CHIP COUNTS ♦

Your starting chip total in a tournament is determined in advance by the tournament director. In low-limit events, a $30 buy-in might give you $500 in chips, though the tournament director could just as easily give you $200 or $1,000.

And in high-limit events, you'll typically receive the same number of chips as the amount of the buy-in. For example, in the main no-limit event of the World Series, players get $10,000 in chips for the $10,000 buy-in. And in WSOP preliminary events that cost, say, $1,000, players get $1,000 in chips.

But there are exceptions. In the WPT $25,000 buy-in championship events at the Bellagio, players received $50,000 in chips. At another tournament, players were given $12,000 in tournament chips for the $10,000 buy-in. At yet another, a $10,000 buy-in netted players $20,000 in starting chips. So, as you see, there are many variations.

However, whether you are given $200 in chips, $1,000 in chips, or $10,000 in chips, you are on a level playing field with your competitors because in a tournament, everyone starts with the same amount of chips. It will then be up to your skill in playing and how you work your luck to see how far you make it into the tournament.

♦ TOURNAMENT CHIPS ♦

Unlike a cash game, where chips are the exact equivalent of money, tournament chips have no cash value. They may just as well be Monopoly money, because no one is going to give you anything for them outside the tournament. Thus, if you have accumulated $150,000 in chips and try to cash them out, all you'll get from the casino is strange looks and an explanation that all you have are tournament chips.

♦ TOURNAMENT PRIZE POOL ♦

The prize pool in tournaments is collected from the total amount of money put up by the players as entry fees. For example, if 200 players compete in a $100 buy-in event, then there is $20,000 available as prize money. Sometimes, the organizers will take a few percentage points off the top for their rake and to distribute as dealer tips. Other times they add on an extra amount to the entry fee to be used for the same purpose. For example, a casino might run a $500 tournament, but charge the players $540. Five hundred dollars goes directly to the prize pool, and the extra $40 is divvied up among the staff. Either way, the house cut will be posted.

Most tournaments are set up so that approximately 10% to 20% of entrants will win cash prizes. For example, if the size of the starting field is 300 players, the organizers might limit the cash payouts to the top 30 finishers (10% of the field). Often, the payout will be rounded down to the number of full tables remaining so if a 300-person tournament was being played nine-handed, the event may pay the top three tables, or twenty-seven players. Some tournaments, such as ones run by the Bellagio, pay out 100 places if they get more than 400 players—which is 25% of the field.

Broader payout schedules are preferable because your chances of getting into the prize money are that much better. Some pros don't like payouts greater than 10% or 15% of the field because the first place prize is reduced. But more winners means more happy players, which is good for the game. And the way I look at it, when the first place prize is well over a million dollars, $100,000 here or there won't be missed too badly by the guy on top, while the guys at the bottom are very thankful for receiving prize money they otherwise would not have won.

In most tournaments, just getting to the final table will earn you prize money. In smaller tournaments under 50 players, you may need to finish among the top three or five players to get prize money First place, of course, will be the biggest prize, followed in order, by second, third, and so on, down to the last paid place, which usually returns what you paid to enter, plus a little more. The first place prize for a larger tournament is usually about a third of the total prize pool, with the exact amount varying according to the tournament setup. Second place often gets half the amount of the winner. That will account for about half the prize money in the tournament, The other half of the prize pool is divided among the remaining winners, with the final table players getting more than players who finish lower down.

The payout structure is usually posted soon after the tournament begins, as the organizers add up the total number of entrants and figure out the number of places and amount paid to each money-winner.

If the structure will affect your decision to play, or if your curiosity can't wait the few minutes to the start time, you can approach the tournament director, and he'll have a good idea of the number of places to be paid. Most players simply wait until the announcement is made by the tournament director or posted on the television monitors (see below) that are typically placed in a location easily visible to the players.

You can determine if the event is right for you by the entry fee and the potential prize pool. The greater the number of players, the bigger the prize pool. When the events are large, such as the $10,000 buy-in events, the prize pool often gets into the millions. These tournaments draw the top players you see on television, along with the amateurs trying their hand at winning the big money.

♦ TELEVISION MONITORS ♦

Most tournaments keep television monitors posted in the tournament area so that you can monitor the progress of the event. They display the level of play, amount of blinds and antes, the number of places being paid, the amount awarded for each finish, and the blind and ante structure for the upcoming round. The fun part of these monitors is the **magic number**, the number of players remaining in the tournament. It is great fun to scoreboard-watch as the event progresses, seeing the number of active players dwindle as others get busted out. The *really* fun part is when you approach the bubble, and realize that, if you can hang in there a bit longer, you'll make it into the money!

♦ THE BUBBLE ♦

In every tournament there comes a point at which one more eliminated player will guarantee payouts for all remaining players. This is called being **on the bubble**. So if you're player number twenty-eight in a tournament paying twenty-seven places, then you've achieved the dubious distinction of being caught on the bubble and going home empty handed, while every remaining player fights on to go deeper into the tournament and win the bigger payouts.

♦ IN-YOUR-SEAT TOURNAMENT RULE ♦

Though tournaments vary slightly in this rule, in general, for your hand to be valid, you must be seated in your chair when the two cards are dealt to your position. If you're not, your hand will be considered dead. Players sometimes get up and stretch or wander over to other tables to check out the action, but if the cards arrive before you do, it's too late. The dealer will disallow play for that hand and collect your cards—hand over.

In the beginning of tournaments, when the tournament director announces to the players, "All players take their seats," and to the dealers, "Shuffle up and deal," you'll sometimes find delinquent players who will forfeit their blinds, sometimes for a few levels of play. Some well-known pros are notorious for showing up in big events hours after the tournament has begun. With the blinds relatively small in the first few rounds, tardy players can get away with losing a few chips since they make only a relatively small dent in their stacks. Later on, however, when the blinds get large, these pros wouldn't dare a long absence from the table as large chip losses could prove critical to their survival.

♦ GETTING COMFORTABLE ♦

If you're comfortable playing cash-game poker, have no worries about mixing it up in tournaments. You'll find the game play virtually identical. The big differences are that the blinds and antes go up as you get deeper into an event and when you bust out, you're finished. Game over. Otherwise, poker is poker.

And with tournaments being so exciting, you won't want to waste too much time before you sit down and take your chance at getting pocket aces on your very first hand—and riding those pocket rockets all the way to the final table!

13. TOURNAMENT NO-LIMIT HOLD'EM STRATEGY

Tournaments are designed to exert increasing pressure on players through growing blinds and antes. Fast tournaments, set up for one evening's play, may change the levels every 15 or 20 minutes, while big buy-in world-class events have rounds of 90 minutes to two hours and are set up to last two days to as long as ten days or more (as in the main event of the World Series of Poker, the $10,000 buy-in no-limit hold'em championship).

All of these structures work the same way. Each level costs players more money in blinds, and after a while, antes, increasing pressure on them to make moves so that these forced bets don't destroy their bankrolls. If you sit out hand after hand, especially as you get to the higher levels, you'll go broke quickly if you're sitting there with short and medium stacks.

Chips are your lifeblood. Everything revolves around how many you have. If you don't have any, nothing revolves around anything, you're dead, and out of the tournament. And if you have a lot of them, you're in very good position to finish near the top, or perhaps on top. And that is what it's all about.

While the ultimate goal is to be the winner of the tournament, if you're able to get *in the money*, that would be a tremendous achievement as a beginning player. The higher up you finish, the more money you get.

♦ TOURNAMENT STRATEGY: THE FOUR STAGES ♦

Tournaments can be divided into four stages: early, middle, late, and final table. Your goals throughout are to increase your chip count and, of course, to survive. While you would like to grow your chip stack after every round, you should not set artificial goals and force play to get there. You can only do what you can do.

Have patience. Situations will present themselves but you have to be around to take advantage of them. The goals I set forth for each of the stages are only general guidelines to shoot for. Again, what will be, will be. But to get to the end, you have to start at the beginning. Following is an overview of a tournament, stage by stage.

Let's start with the early round strategy.

♠ Early Round Tournament Strategy: Surviving

In the first few rounds of a tournament, the blinds are generally small, and the antes often don't kick in until the third or fourth level. During these early rounds, with not much at stake, there is little pressure on you to make any moves or enter even one pot as the blinds won't make too much of a dent in your stack, at least not a critical dent. Your strategy here is to play conservatively, trying to win little pots when possible and avoiding big pots and all-ins unless you think you have the winner. You don't want to risk your tournament on a foolish bluff or by playing speculative or second-best hands for too many chips.

In these early rounds, you don't want to lose a significant portion of your chips or your entire stack trying to win a few hundred. Later, when the blinds are significant and you need the chips, you may take more chances in the right situation. But early on, survive and wait for your trap hands. Still, you'll typically find at least one player who will go broke within ten minutes, even at the major championships. And by the time the early rounds are over, more than one-fifth of the field will be gone.

Your goal is to increase your chips stack as the tournament progresses. Hopefully you can double up after three rounds, but don't force the action. Play your cards and the situations—don't be driven by what you'd like to happen. If you've maintained an average chip count, you're still very much in the game. And that's a lot better than being very much out of the game.

♠ Middle Round Tournament Strategy: Getting Positioned

In the middle rounds of a tournament, around levels four to eight, players get eliminated at a more rapid rate. The blinds and antes start taking big chunks out of your bankroll, and each round of play removes more leverage from your stack. This means you need to take more chances to maintain the health of your chip stack and to avoid getting eliminated. For players whose chips have dwindled, the pressure is on and they have to start gambling to survive.

The middle stages are not just about playing defensively, but going on the attack. It is time to go after the blinds and antes more aggressively because there are more chips to be won. Build up your stack if you can. Chips are power, and the more of them you have, the better off you are.

And since no-limit is a game of leverage, you always want to make sure you have enough chips in your stack so that when you make a bet, it gets the respect it deserves. And if that bet is an all-in, it has to have enough weight to intimidate opponents and make them think very carefully about whether they want to call it. When your chip stack gets too low, your bets will scare no one and you have lost your biggest weapon in no-limit: intimidation.

Look out for players protecting their stacks and go after them. If you get fortunate enough to trap an opponent and become one of the big stacks, smaller-stacked opponents will be wary of messing with you, giving you more opportunities to push players around.

If you're short-stacked, you have to steal blinds and play aggressive poker in order to keep up with the costs of blinds and antes. And if you get to a danger point—with a stack less than five times the size of the big blind—you need to look for opportunities to move all your chips into the middle. If you're big-stacked, you want to push around the weak players and small stacks to get more chips. You're looking to position yourself for the final table.

If you can survive these rounds, you're almost in the money. Many players will be eliminated, probably one-third to one half the number who started, so you've made real progress. In a big event, the $5,000 or higher buy-ins, you've made it into the second day. Still, there is a long way to go.

♠ Late Round Tournament Strategy: In the Money

If you've lasted into the later rounds, you've either made it into the money or are getting real close. Now you look forward, hoping to get to the final table and the *big* money. You want to pick up your game here and play your best poker. Avoid facing off in big pots or all-ins against stacks that can take you out—unless you've got the goods—but as always in a tournament, keep pushing your weight around against players that can be bullied.

Once you get into the money, every place higher you finish, or every small number of places (usually table by table), means you get more prize money. You may want to fold marginal hands if lasting one or two more places means a lot more prize money. But at the same time, if you are in a good situation, go for it. If you bust out, so be it. If you make a big play and get a windfall of chips, you've now leapfrogged into position for a much higher finish, and really, when you start getting close, you've got to be thinking big.

Think, "final table, final table, final table," and maybe you'll get there.

♠ Final Table: Looking for the Championship

If you get to the final table, you have a good shot at winning it all, but you still have to get through the last players. If you're among the big stacks, avoid going to war against another big stack that can bust you or make you one of the small stacks—unless you're feeling real good about your hand. Use your big stack to put pressure on smaller stacks struggling to stay alive.

If you're low-stacked, the blinds and antes are exerting tremendous pressure, leaving you with little choice but to find your best opportunity and then go after it for all your chips. Calling is not an option here. If you're low-stacked and have to make a play to avoid being emergency-stacked, put maximum pressure on opponents by betting all your chips on a preflop raise. If you have enough chips to sting opponents—and never let yourself get below that "sting" level—you'll make it hard for opponents to call, which gives you the best chance of walking away with the pot.

Think before you make your moves, keeping in mind that every player eliminated means a huge jump in prize money for the remaining players. You don't get to a final table very often, so when you do, you want to make the most of it. Hopefully, that means the ultimate—you'll be the champion!

♦ 7 ESSENTIAL SKILLS IN NO-LIMIT HOLD'EM TOURNAMENTS ♦

In the seven key strategic concepts chapter, we looked at important fundamentals that apply to all forms of hold'em— limit, no-limit, and pot-limit. These principles apply to both cash games and tournaments. In this section, I'll cover seven concepts that apply specifically to tournament no-limit— surviving, having chips, playing without cards, minimizing bad plays, understanding that chips are power, and knowing when to back down—because they are so important to every form of tournament poker.

I'm also going to reiterate one concept from the seven key strategic concepts chapter, *being aggressive*, because this attribute is essential if you are to succeed in tournament play. Or for that matter, any form of poker.

♦ THE 7 ESSENTIAL SKILLS ♦

1. Surviving

2. Having Chips

3. Playing Without Cards

4. Minimizing Bad Plays

5. Understanding that Chips are Power

6. Knowing When to Back Down

7. Being Aggressive

1. Surviving

In a tournament, your strategy boils down to one thing: survival. That's right, *survival.* Your goal is to hang in there and move up the ladder as players get eliminated so that you can get into the prize money. And finally, you want to get to the final table or be the champion. You must carefully pick your spots, ones that you can win, so that as players get knocked out of action, you stay alive, still in the mix. And as the weak get parted from the herd, you crawl closer to the top.

Remember this: *patience is integral to survival.* You cannot afford critical lapses in judgment. Throwing all your chips into the pot on a foolish bluff or reckless play is the worst thing you can do. In a cash game, you can always go into your pocket for more chips if you get broke. Not so in a tournament. There is no second chance. So you must be patient and wait for your spot to pounce.

If you hang around long enough, you give good situations a chance to find you. Your cards and situations will come along. Just make sure you're around to take advantage of them.

2. Having Chips

You have to have chips. Without them, you have little to win when you catch big hands and everything to lose in confrontations with a bigger stack. Maybe you'll get dealt pocket aces or kings, and get action, with your hand holding up. Perhaps you'll flop a set, or make even a bigger hand, and be able to trap an opponent who will lose to your boss hand. And when these situations occur, you want to have chips, lots of them, so you can win big pots. If you have $1,000 in chips and trap an opponent, the most you can win from him is $1,000. But if you have $7,000 in chips, you have a lot more upside potential.

To maximize your chances of success in no-limit tournaments, you need leverage. You need to have enough chips so that opponents fear your bets, and of course, so you can survive. You never want your chip stack to get so low that you lose the power of the hammer or the ability to win enough chips if all your chips go in the middle.

3. Playing Without Cards

You don't get a lot of good cards in hold'em, so you need to be able to make moves without strong hands. Look for situations where you can outplay opponents and take their chips. Be ready to push opponents off a pot with a big bet and no cards backing you up. It's called a bluff. It's the beauty of poker—and life. You fluff your colorful feathers and hope they don't get clipped.

Players who sit and wait for good cards to play hard don't go far in a tournament. Their play will be predictable and their opportunities to gather chips will be few. No limit hold'em is a situational game. When you sense weakness, use the hammer and pounce. Take an opponent off a pot and take his chips. In other words, play the player.

4. Minimizing Bad Plays

You must minimize bad plays, particularly catastrophic ones that can cripple your stack—or lose it entirely—and really set you back into a trouble zone. Chips are a limited resource and you can only replenish your supply by winning more of them. Sometimes you'll play correctly and lose. That's okay, bad beats are a part of the game and you can't worry about them. But don't cripple your chances or go out of a tournament on a hand you *shouldn't* be playing. Minimize catastrophic plays and you maximize your chances of making a final table—or better.

In no-limit, your entire stack of chips is subject to be risked and lost at any time. So when you do push the big stack of chips in the middle, you want to be fairly confident that you have the best of the situation, that the odds are stacked on your side—and not on your opponent's.

5. Understanding that Chips are Power

In a tournament, chips are power, chips are your blood. If you have a lot of them, take advantage of your superior chip count by bullying short stacks and timid players with aggressive play. Anytime you bet and compete against a smaller stack, he knows that if he goes to war with you for all his chips and loses, he's eliminated. It is difficult for short stacks to play back at you because you can break them. Conversely, when you're that smaller stack, you must tread carefully against bigger stacks because your tournament will be at stake if all the chips go in the middle.

At all times, and certainly before you go into battle, always be aware of your opponents' relative chip status—who's got the big stacks, who's got the average stacks, and who's got the short stacks—and where your stack is at in the pecking order. You need to know which opponents you can bully because you have the dominant stack, and which ones can bully you because they have the dominant stack. If you're the loser in all-in situations against a bigger stack, you get eliminated. However, if your stack is more sizable then your opponent, all you can lose is chips—you'll still be alive to see another hand.

♠ TIP ♠

Always keep this in mind: when you have fewer chips than an opponent, he can take you out if all the chips get in the middle; when you have more, you can take him out.

---

6. Knowing When to Back Down

You have to know when to back down from a hand that you think is pretty good—but might not be the best—and give up the pot. It doesn't matter how good your hand is. It only matters whether it is *better* than your opponent's hand. You must have the guts *and* the ability to lay down a big hand against a lot of betting pressure. Players that don't heed warning signs take big hits in cash games and have early exits in tournaments.

If it looks like you're in big trouble on a hand, don't be afraid to let your cards go. Marriage (to your cards) may not be forever, but death (losing all your chips) is. You're referred back to concept number one: survival.

7. Being Aggressive

Winning is always about aggression. Aggressive betting gives you two ways to win pots. Either your opponents will back off the pot and give it to you, or they call and get pounded even harder on the next card. If they call all the way down to the river and find out that they've been barking up against a monster, they're in trouble. That's a chance most players will not be willing to take unless they're fairly certain they have you beaten. Bets and raises make opponents think about messing with you. And it makes them think about folding. Advantage: the player betting and raising. Disadvantage: the opponent watching you collect their chips.

♦ YOUR CHIP STACK ♦

To be a winner in no-limit hold'em tournaments, you must quickly integrate the concept that every professional player intuitively understands: it is not how you play your cards, but how you play your chips! The number of chips you have relative to the big blind and your opponents is a factor in every decision you make. When you're short on chips, there is greater pressure on you to make moves to stay alive—and every opponent will be aware of this. And when you're awash in chips, you can exert greater pressure on opponents who want to stay out of confrontations with you that can take them out of the tournament. You have the luxury of being patient and choosing the spots that best suit your situation. A few rounds of attrition from blinds and antes won't make a serious dent in your stack.

> ## ♠ KEY TOURNAMENT CONCEPT ♠
>
> It is not how you play your cards, but how you play your chips!

Ideally, you would like your stack to be *at least* twenty-five times the size of the big blind. This is your **minimum ideal stack** size. You have enough chips to play pressure-free poker without worrying too much about being blinded out. Sometimes your chips get low and the pressure-cooker is on the stove. Or worse, your chips might get really low and the situation becomes critical. Other times, you'll be a big stack, with the advantage of leverage against smaller stacks just trying to survive.

Your chip stack influences so much of your strategy that it can never be ignored. In a tournament, it's all about the chips. Let's take a further look at how the size of your chip stack affects *everything*.

> ## ♠ CHIPS ♠
>
> It's all about the chips. Chips are survival. Chips are power. You need to have enough chips to survive, and you need lots of chips to prosper.

♠ Playing Short Stacks

If you have less than ten times the big blind in your tournament stack, then you have a **short stack** and must play more aggressively to grow your stack. You don't have the luxury of waiting for good cards forever. By doing nothing but folding, every set of deals around the table costs you the equivalent of about two big blind bets. And if you're starting with only ten big blinds, one round means you're down to about eight big blinds and in two rounds you're almost cut in half and down to about six big blinds!

You can see where this is going. If you wait too long to make a move, you will soon get **blinded off**—lose all or most of your chips to the blinds and antes without even playing a hand. At the same time, as a short stack, you are perilously close to having one big loss either crippling your stack or eliminating you altogether.

The additional problems you face as a short stack have to do with a loss of leverage:

1. Opponents give your bets less respect and are more likely to call you down with less than premium hands when you move chips into the middle. There are three reasons for this:

a. Knowing that you have to make a move, opponents give you less credit for strong hands.

b. Your potential of bringing down the hammer—putting a big intimidating bet in front of you—is minimized because you don't have enough chips to really hurt them.

c. The threat of them putting the hammer to you gives them the edge because a bigger stack would only be risking chips; you'd be risking your entire tournament.

2. Opponents are more likely to bet and raise against you. When your stack is desperately low, you'll play all sorts of hands (as would your opponents). Your opponents will know this, so they'll be more likely to call your bets with weaker hands.

3. For all the reasons above, you'll be less likely to run a successful bluff.

♠ Attrition Rate when there are Antes and Blinds

Every set of deals around the table costs the equivalent of about two big blind bets.

The attrition is fast and harsh once the antes kick in and you're short-stacked. Patience is no longer your buzzword. You're now thinking of *action*, in the right situation and at the right time.

With a short stack, you become more dependent on finding and taking advantage of the right situation because you have less time to wait for premium cards and big flops. You have to start taking more risks to get chips. This doesn't mean that you should play recklessly—that is never a good idea—but if the cards don't come, you've got to go out there and make something happen.

Winning pots if the right cards or situations come along, or stealing blinds or flops if they don't, should be right on top of your list. But like always, think *aggression*.

Beginners make the mistake of limping in pots with low stacks or calling all-ins with inferior hands. As a low stack, you want to make the big move *first* and put the decision to your opponents. Limping in with a third of your chips allows opponents to call with hands they may have folded against a bigger bet. Make the big move when you have to make the big move. It's your only chance. And by moving with *all* your chips, you maintain enough leverage to give opponents pause when considering whether to call your hand.

♠ Playing With Emergency Short Stacks

Let's say the antes are $25 and the blinds are $50/$100 in a ten-handed game. You're sitting with $500 in chips. One round of deals goes by and you don't play a hand. Here is what happens. You lose ten antes at $25 each (for $250 total), plus a small blind at $50 and a big blind at $100 means. In just ten hands, $400 will be eaten up, leaving you $100—barely anything.

Obviously, you can't let this happen. You've got to make a play before that $500 in chips go away; in other words, *immediately*. If you don't get chips quickly, you're a goner in one and half rounds of play, tops.

When your chip count is five-times the size of the big blind or less—what I call an **emergency short-stack**—you're in trouble, and must be ready to pounce with all your power at the very first decent opportunity. You have to pick up the blinds and antes to stay alive. It's your food for survival. To give yourself the best chance of getting those chips, you need to use all the leverage you have available. You cannot afford to play passive here—calling is not an option, nor is a standard raise—the all-in bet is your *only* move.

You need to make a play before the blinds drop you a notch lower, and if possible, you want to have some value in your hand. If the pot is unraised and you are dealt any pair, ace-any (an ace with any other card), or any two cards 10 or higher, push in all your chips and hope for the best. Quite often you'll get no callers and the blinds and antes that you win will give you enough fuel for another round of play.

If the pot is raised before you by a player who's tight or looks strong, you might wait out a hand or two unless you think you have better.

You're in survival mode and must pick a situation you can win. That means you're holding the best hand and win with the best cards or you don't have the best hand and hope to win the pot without a fight. If you have to, you'll make your move with *any* two cards. Keep this in mind: if you have 7-2 and go head-to-head against an opponent with an A-K, you're only about a 2 to 1 underdog. So you always have a chance.

And you want to make your play while you still have some chips behind you. This is extremely important. Better to play

7-2 with $500 to win than 7-2 with only $100 chips to win. In the first instance, you'll be up to $1,000 and have more breathing room before you come hard at the pot again. And you have a little bit of leverage. In the second instance, you'll have no leverage, and if you do win, you get so little that you haven't improved your situation. You need chips and must make your play while you have something to win and while you have enough chips so that if your opponents buck heads against you, they have something to lose!

The clock is ticking fast when you've got an emergency low stack, and you might get only one good shot, so pick your best situation and go for it. You may have to go after the pot with any two cards. May the chips be with you.

♠ Playing Average Stacks

Having an **average stack**—about equal to the average amount of chips held by players—means you're right in the center of things. You have enough chips to be patient and wait for your opportunities. In other words, you can play your best poker without undue pressure. Just like the big stacks, you want to avoid major confrontations against other average stacks or big stacks unless you've got the best hand. Good players with chips will avoid confrontations with you as well so there will be bluffing opportunities, but again, don't lose chips to foolish moves.

As always, smaller stacks are your targets. Push them around and get chips from them. If bigger stacks play weak, don't be afraid to exert pressure on them as well. Look for chips wherever you can get them and from whomever will give them to you.

♠ Playing Big Stacks

Having a **big stack** means you have more than double the average amount of chips in play. You have a big advantage as a big stack. You can afford to lose big pots and still have chips to play, particularly against small stacks. This doesn't mean you want to lose big pots—which can come as a result of a huge mistake or from a bad beat (and those can't be helped)—only that you can afford a bad break and still be alive. This is a luxury smaller stacks do not have.

As a big stack, you can pressure players trying to stay alive by betting aggressively, especially against players who are playing scared or are short-stacked. You want to avoid other big stacks unless you have the best hand. This goes for average stacks as well, because a big confrontation with an average stack can make him the big stack and you the average one—or smaller.

Players fear big stacks, especially aggressive big stacks who are willing to push chips into the middle. When you sense weakness in an opponent, pounce on it. Stealing blinds, aggressive flop betting, and reraising are very effective weapons. However, do not foolishly throw away chips just because you have a lot of them. Whatever good play got you the big stack, keep it going to maintain and increase your position. A big stack has leverage, but use that leverage wisely.

Let's now talk about how you can earn those chips.

♠ STACK SIZES ♠

Chip Stack	Stack Size	Strategy
Emergency Short	5x big blind	All-in first good situation
Short	10x big blind	All-in is only bet
Medium (Average)	Average stack	Play to style
Minimum Ideal	25x big blind	Play to style
Large	2x average stack	Step up aggression. Find opponents who play scared and pound them

♦ SEVEN WEAPONS TO EARN CHIPS IN NO-LIMIT ♦

In tournaments, you not only need to win chips to keep up with the steady loss of chips to the blind and antes that constantly erode your stack, but to keep up with the greater number of chips held by the average player as the tournament goes deeper and deeper and the field thins. Tournaments start with a set amount of chips, and from start to finish, when there is one player left, the total number of chips neither decreases nor increases. It remains constant, only fewer players hold the same amount of "wealth."

As players get eliminated, these chips gets spread among fewer players. For example, if you start out with $1,000 in chips in a field of 100 players, that's $100,000 of total chips in play. If 50 players get eliminated, the average stack doubles, with each player averaging $2,000 in chips. Of course, some will have more, and a few many more, and some will have less, with others having emergency low stacks and hovering on the brink of elimination. But there's still that same $100,000 of total chips in play. If you've remained static at about $1,000, you're behind the curve.

So it's not just about keeping up with the blinds and antes so that your stack remains constant. Sitting on your nest and hatching eggs just won't do. You need to grow your stack. Of course, you can't force the action and increase your chips just because you want to. You can only do your best given the circumstances and cards that present themselves. If you're behind the curve, don't worry, opportunities will come along to gather more, and hopefully these will be ones in which you'll prevail and win chips.

Unless you're short-stacked and have to make a big move, patience is a virtue. You've got time, use it to your advantage.

These are the main weapons you'll use to win chips in no-limit hold tournaments: (Note that many of these methods apply equally to limit and pot-limit hold'em tournaments and cash games.)

♦ SEVEN WEAPONS TO EARN CHIPS IN NO-LIMIT ♦

1. Stealing Blinds (and Antes)

2. Restealing

3. Betting the Flop

4. Take Advantage of the Bubble

5. Using the Hammer

6. The Trap

7. Aggression

1. Stealing Blinds (and antes)

Stealing of blinds and antes on the preflop is the bread and butter of your hold'em arsenal and a great way to replenish your chip stack. Without picking up other players blinds, you're going to have a hard time surviving. You need those chips to replenish your own loss of chips to the blinds and antes. You don't get many good hands to play, so while you wait for good cards to come, you need to occasionally steal blinds holding nothing; in other words, on a pure bluff.

The best positions to steal blinds from are the button or the seat before the button. Use the power of late position to raise three times the big blind and hopefully force the blinds and later position players out of the pot. Often, the blinds will fold, giving you the pot uncontested. You don't want to make this play every time, because your opponents will catch on and spank you back with a reraise forcing you to fold, but at the same time, if the blinds are going to give you the pot without a fight, well then, take it every time.

2. Restealing

Late position players, and sometime middle or early position players, are going to steal blinds. When you get a good feeling that they're going after the blinds, make a pot-sized reraise. If they are on a steal or playing a weak hand, they'll fold and give you the pot. That's called a **resteal**. It's a bolder play than the steal because it requires you to put more chips at risk, and there's always the chance that your opponent has a legitimate hand. But in poker, there's always the chance that anything could occur—almost nothing is for sure. You can't play scared and hope to win in this game.

The resteal puts lots of pressure on your opponent and gives him plenty of reasons to fold. When it works, it's even better than the steal because you have won not only the blinds, but your opponent's raise as well!

3. Betting the Flop

Again: aggression, aggression, aggression. Betting and raising wins chips. Take the lead and come out betting the flop. More times than not, that pot will be yours. But don't overuse this play to the point that everyone knows you're going to make the move. If you become too predictable, aggressive opponents will come over the top of you and take your chips away.

Going after flops aggressively, no matter what three cards appear, will win you many pots, especially against tight players.

4. Take Advantage of the Bubble

Everyone wants to win money. And everyone wants the prestige of finishing *in the money*. But to do so, you have to clear the bubble. When you're close, you don't want to be the player to bust out on the bubble with the money going to *everyone else*. As a result, play slows down and almost everyone gets very conservative, just waiting for one small stack to bust out.

That is, *almost* everyone. If you've got enough chips to play with, this is the time to step up your game and steal and resteal while the rest of the crowd hangs on to clear the bubble. The bubble presents a golden opportunity to stockpile chips.

5. Using the Hammer

Big bets and all-in bets put a lot of pressure on smaller stacks. There is even pressure on bigger stacks as well. No one wants to lose a big pot, especially smaller stacks who will go bye-bye if they play for all their chips and lose. Use the hammer of the big bet at the right times, and you'll take chips away. And if opponents fear your hammer, they'll be more likely to get out of your way even when you just tip-toe into the pot.

Find the weak opponents and blast away at them with aggressive bets that they'll have a hard time calling.

6. The Trap

Big pots are won in no-limit hold'em by trapping an opponent. The best time to set a trap is when you get a big hand and your opponent also has a big hand, but a lesser one. For example, say you hold aces against an opponent's kings, and all the chips find their way into the middle before the flop.

Or you could have a huge disguised hand against an opponent who has no clue that you're holding a monster—so you've got a trap set up. Get as many chips into the pot as you can in this situation. You might be up against an aggressive player who pushes his luck too far, or one who thinks he's leading your horse to the water, and doesn't realize that you're holding a big hand and the oasis is yours, not his. Sometimes, you're fortunate, and all the chips get in the middle without much work. Other times you have to be sneaky and have the right cards drop. You have to figure out how best to shake the coconuts from your opponent's tree—and hopefully all of them.

But to set the most effective trap, you need to have enough chips to win enough chips. And hopefully your opponent also has enough chips to really make the hand a windfall for you.

A trap hand will show up for you, but again, you've got to be around to take advantage of it. Hands don't come when you're on the rail, nor do they help you much when you don't have much to win. So don't panic and go out on bad hands just because it looks like you're cold-decked and you feel like you need to make a big play. Hang around, good things will happen.

7. Aggression

There's that word again—aggression. To win at poker, particularly the no-limit varieties, you have to be aggressive. The worst thing you can do in no-limit hold'em tournaments is turn into a **calling station**, a player who calls bets and rarely raises. Reread the above six no-limit tournament weapons. They all have one element in common—aggressive betting.

Remember this: the player who wins the chips is usually the player who goes after them.

♠ KEY CONCEPT:
YOU WANT TO BE BLUFFED! ♠

It is better to be wrong by folding and be bluffed out of some chips, than to be wrong by calling and get taken out of the tournament. Have chips, have life.

♦ REBUY AND ADD-ON TOURNAMENTS: STRATEGY ♦

Rebuy and add-on tournaments give you a chance to purchase more chips in the first few rounds. This changes the nature of hands you might play because you have the opportunity to "get another chance." (If only life was always like that, no?)

Each rebuy or add-on costs money. The question is, "Does it make sense to invest more money into the tournament?" Let's look at that now.

During the rebuy period in unlimited rebuy tournaments you could theoretically bust out after every hand and then rebuy for more chips. That can get expensive and make the cost of playing a low-buy-in tournament not so low-cost anymore. And the same goes for medium and high buy-in tournaments, where the original buy-in may turn out to be a mere fraction of the overall cost you end up paying.

For example, let's say you pay $30 to enter an unlimited rebuy tournament which allows a double add-on at the end of the rebuy period, and the cost of each rebuy and add-on is $30. To keep yourself on an even playing field, you have to walk into the event with a bankroll of no less than $90. The first $30 is for the entry fee, and the next $60 is for the double add-on. If you plan on purchasing two to three rebuys, then you need to budget an extra $60 to $90. So your entry fee is not really $30—that's only your initial *deposit*—but $90 to $180, depending upon the number of rebuys you purchase.

A reasonable approach to rebuy tournaments is to limit yourself to two or three rebuys. If you bust out after this, you can figure that it's just not your day and move on. And if you do well, you must be prepared to invest more to protect your investment.

In a tournament, a player with a lot of chips has a tremendous advantage over another player with less. When the rebuy period ends and you are given the option to increase your chip total with an add-on, you'll generally want to take advantage of this opportunity. If you have tripled your original chip count, you can consider riding with what you have, but even there, adding on for more gives you more power and a better chance to win.

Let's say you start a tournament with $1,000 in chips, build it up to $1,750, and decline an add-on at the end of the rebuy period. You will be at a tremendous disadvantage to a player who has that same $1,750 and picks up a $1,000 add-on to bring his stack to $2,750. And if it's a double add-on, a player with a stack of $3,750 has a giant edge over you.

You cannot enter a rebuy tournament without being prepared to take on the additional costs of the add-ons. Not if you want to keep the playing field level and give yourself the best chance of winning. You simply must have enough money to purchase the add-ons available. You may decline to do rebuys and call your tournament finished if you bust-out—or at least limit your rebuys to one or two times—but if you're still in there when it's time to add-on, you have to be able to compete. And that means having enough money for an add-on *and* taking advantage of the opportunity to get more chips.

You have more leverage over opponents when your risk of losing a big pot and being crippled is less than them. You also can't bust out against an opponent when you have more chips than he has. It's the law of the land in tournaments: big stacks rule the jungle.

14. PLAYING THE PLAYERS

Poker is a game played against people. It is about psychology, trying to deceive opponents about the strength of your hand or lack of, and at the same time, trying to ascertain the strength of theirs. It is about inducing opponents to either fold when you bet so you can win the pot right there, or to put more money into a pot you believe you'll win.

In every situation, figuring out how to play a hand depends on how you think your opponents will react to your checks, calls, bets, and raises. And part of that thinking process is determining how you think *they* think you're going to react to *their* betting actions. That's how it works at the poker table; while you're trying to figure them out, they're trying to figure you out. Spy versus spy.

In other words, it's all about playing the player. Learning how to adjust for various types of players is a key ingredient to being a winning Texas hold'em player.

♦ PLAYING TENDENCIES ♦

Seeing an opponent's playing tendencies—conservative or aggressive, loose or tight, big bluffer or not a bluffer—is obvious to everyone, regardless of experience. Any player, whether a rank beginner or a seasoned expert, can quickly and easily see whether an opponent plays a lot of hands or plays few, and whether he tends to call or raise.

At the table, it doesn't take long for a player to reveal his playing style. And once you have an idea of your opponents' styles, you can adjust your own play to maximize your results. Playing styles can be categorized into one of four fundamental types; conservative, aggressive, loose, and tight. There are substyles as well, but these main categories will give you a general sense of the types of opponents you'll face.

Let's take a closer look at them.

1. PLAYING AGAINST LOOSE PLAYERS

Loose players love action. They play too many hands, call too many bets, and stay in pots too long. By playing more hands, they will win more pots, but at the expense of too many bets when they lose. Net result: overall losses—unless they're a world class player who can get away with this type of play. Since loose players play more hands, their cards will be weaker, on average, than your typical non-loose opponent. So you need to adjust.

When you're in pots against loose players:

1. Call more often at the showdown, since they'll get there with weaker cards.

2. Don't try to move them off of pots when you have nothing. Bluffing just won't work against players who'll call with any hope in their hand.

3. Play more marginal hands than usual when you're heads-up, since their average hand will be weaker. However, stick to a fundamentally solid approach. Don't get drawn into a loose player's game.

Let loose players win their pots. You like to see that. The more they win, the more they have for you to get. When you're in there against them with a big hand, you'll make them pay a hefty price for playing weaker cards to the end.

2. PLAYING AGAINST TIGHT PLAYERS

Tight players enter few pots and only with premium hands. Against them you need to loosen up your game. Play more aggressively against tight players since they'll more readily give up the pot. When you bet or raise them, they'll usually fold marginal hands. This means you can easily push them out of pots with any garbage you hold—your cards are irrelevant when an opponent won't defend his hand. When you're playing hold'em, particularly no-limit, you'll want to consistently attack their blinds, which they won't defend.

Take advantage of tight opponents by always figuring them for a good hand when they're in the pot. Respect their bets; they're generally betting on solid cards. In borderline situations, give tight players the benefit of the doubt and call their bets less often. When you do call their bets, call with cards you figure can win. And if a tight player raises, make sure the pot odds and the strength of your hand justify a call, because he probably has cards worth betting on.

Since tight players won't play mediocre hands, you can force them out of the pot early with strong bets. If your hand is mediocre and a tight opponent bets, give him credit for strength and save your chips.

Note that tight players can be either conservative or aggressive.

3. PLAYING AGAINST CONSERVATIVE PLAYERS

Conservative players play non-aggressive poker— tending to call rather than raise and check rather than bet.

They put little pressure on opponents. This style of play tends to be very predictable and keeps the level of risk relatively low for their opponents. In Texas hold'em, you need to protect your good hands so that the field is narrowed, and your good hands hold up to be winners.

The advantage of playing against conservative players is that you get to see more cards for free or at least cheaply. Marginal hands are more valuable because you'll be able to see more cards with them, and if you hit your hand, you're going to win chips you'd otherwise have no shot at. Conservative players make big mistakes when they let opponents into a pot when they should be shutting them out. The more hands an opponent lets you sneak in on, the more vulnerable that player is to having pots taken away from him—sometimes, big pots.

In general, you want to up your aggression against conservative players. This will allow you to more frequently drive them out of pots even when you have inferior hands because they are less likely to defend those pots unless they have strong cards. If they happen to be playing behind you, steal their blinds by raising every time they allow you to. No-limit hold'em is the wrong game for conservative players and if you're lucky enough to get in hands against these kinds of opponents, you'll get extra opportunities to win chips.

4. PLAYING AGAINST AGGRESSIVE PLAYERS

Aggressive players keep the heat on during a game. They bet and raise frequently, so getting involved in a hand with them is going to cost you chips. Aggressive players take advantage of opponents' tendencies to fold rather than put more chips into the pot, and they'll keep pushing at pots with hands that don't support such heavy betting.

When you mix it up with aggressive players, you know

they're going to pound you with bets and raises. So you've got to be ready to commit chips if you're going to play a pot against them. To counteract their style, you have to fight fire with fire and be prepared to raise their bets, or reraise their raises. If they've got nothing, which will often be the case, you'll be able to take that pot. Of course, you have to make good reads when you're committing chips because aggressive players won't always have nothing. But at the same time, you can't let players push you around.

Aggressive players will throw lots of chips around so slowing down your game when you get a big hand can pay big dividends. The aggressive opponent will build the pot for you while your passive play disguises the strength of your hand. This leaves the too-forward player vulnerable to a very big loss.

♦ TELLS: THE BODY LANGUAGE OF POKER ♦

In poker, the body language, expressions, or mannerisms that reveal the strength or weakness of a player's cards are called **tells**. There are two types of tells—physical ones described below, and betting pattern tells, in which the amount a player bets—and under what circumstances—reveals information on the hand he's holding.

♠ Eleven Key Tells

There are tons of tells, some that are common among novice players and others that are particular to individual players. It is always important to carefully observe your opponents, not just for their style of play and betting tendencies, but for tells that can help you determine the best way to play against them.

Here are eleven basic tells that will help you get an edge on opponents.

1. Players who act strong are often weak. Players talking loudly or betting in an aggressive manner would like you to believe that they've got the goods.

2. Players who act weak are often strong. As above, look for opposites. Watch out for a player who looks like he is reluctantly tossing his chips into the middle. He's got a strong hand.

3. Players who grab their chips as if they're going to bet while you contemplate your betting action. They're trying to intimidate you into not betting if you're leading into the action—or not raising if a bet has already been placed—so that they can come into the pot for free or at least, cheaply. Or, if they have led out with a bet, for you to fold.

4. Players who look at you when they bet or even stare you down. It's an intimidation tactic to get you to fold or not bet. Think item #1 on this list; acting strong when weak.

5. Players who look at their chips when new cards are revealed on the board. Subconsciously, they're thinking about the chips they want to bet, meaning they've got a hand worth betting on, probably a strong one.

6. Players who look at the pot when new cards are revealed. Ditto above. They're subconsciously counting chips for a pot they figure to win.

7. Players who watch your chips while awaiting your betting action. They're nervous about a potential bet from you because they're weak.

8. Player who are unnaturally quiet when they're in a hand. Look for strength.

9. Players who appear more nervous or excited than usual when they're involved in a hand. They're not nervous because they have a weak hand, but because they're strong!

10. Players who appear to be frozen after betting and are awaiting an opponent's reaction. They're bluffing.

11. Players that look at their cards again often don't remember what they have. What does this mean? Their cards are not that strong or they would remember.

Note that while most tells are the real deal—subconscious mannerisms that are telltale signs you can use to your advantage—some players may consciously show a fake tell in an attempt to fool you. So beware: don't put 100% stock into tells because they're not always reliable. First and foremost, always use your poker knowledge and intuition as the main guideline for making strategy decisions. If you think you have a tell on an opponent, use that to influence your decision, but only if you're more than reasonably certain that the tell is legitimate.

Tells can provide valuable information, especially with beginning players and at low-limit tables, but like every other decision in the game of poker, always consider all the information at hand before you choose an action.*

---

* The classic book on tells, *Caro's Book of Poker Tells* by Mike Caro, is required reading if you wish to look deeper into the subject.

15. ONLINE POKER

It is a brand new world out there. Online poker is hot with millions of players around the world competing against one another on hundreds of sites! With a few clicks of your mouse, you can get in on the action too. Most sites allow you to play for free so you can get accustomed to their software. Or you can sign up and play for real money.

There are many online sites with a great choice of games and limits. If you're a low-limit dollar player, a higher-limit $50/$100 player, or even a penny-ante player, take heart. There are games available. Whether you like cash games or tournaments, low stakes or high stakes, or simply playing for free, it is all available on the Internet, and the games are ongoing 24/7. You can have great fun playing online and you can make money as well.

What's not to like?

♦ GETTING STARTED ♦

Playing poker online is easy once you get the software loaded up on your computer and get money into your account. But these two steps require some patience, as they are not quite so easy as snapping your fingers and diving right in.

There are five steps to complete before you can started.

1. Find a site you wish to play on.

2. Download the software onto your computer.

3. Learn the basic functions of the site.

4. Get money into your account.

5. Start playing!

Let's take a brief look at each of the five steps, beginning with the most basic one of all: where to play!

1. Find a site you wish to play on.

There are hundreds of sites to choose from. These sites are licensed in various countries around the world, with reputations that range from spotless to disreputable. Generally speaking, online poker sites are relatively trouble-free and for a very good reason—there's just too much money being made by online poker rooms to do anything but deal an honest game and make customers happy.

For the latest information on the best online poker rooms (and the ones to avoid), go to our website: **www.cardozapub.com**.

2. Download the software.

Once you have chosen a site and gone to its homepage, you will be provided with step-by-step instructions for all the basics: how to set up a unique account and password, how to play for free, and how to deposit funds into your account so that you can play for real money. If you're a bit unfamiliar and uncomfortable with the processes, don't worry. The instructions are pretty straightforward. If you are familiar with downloading, it's pretty easy; all you're doing is following the site's instructions. Click, click, click. Soon you'll have the poker software on your computer. Easy!

3. Learn the basic functions and options of the site.

On every site, you'll always enter and start on the home page. From there you'll be able to choose the different things you want to do: log on using your screen name and password, get instructions for depositing money and playing, learn about any bonuses and specials, move money in and out of a game, and of course, go to an area where you can choose a cash game or tournament, and the limit you wish to play. All these options will be carefully explained in the site's instructions.

Once you know how to play online poker on one site, you'll pretty much know how to play on all of the online poker rooms as the features are similar.

To be extra safe when you enter a site for the first time, you may want to play a few free games so that you get comfortable with the site's playing and betting interface and can get your feet wet without cost or risk. And only then should you play for money.

Aha, let's see about that now.

4. Get money into your account.

If you just want to play for fun, with no monetary risk, then skip this step. But if you want to gamble—be it for pennies or thousands of dollars, then you first need to get the loot to the site.

I'd like to tell you that getting money into your account is a snap, a gum chew, and a walk, but it's a little harder than that; you have to clear a few hurdles first. This might take a few days or longer, so if you suddenly get the bug for real-money play, you're just going to have to wait until you get money deposited into your account—and that money has to be cleared and become available to you. It may take a few days, possibly even a week, depending on the payment method you use.

Given that most online poker rooms cannot accept credit

card deposits (at least not from their American and Canadian-based customers), many sites use NETeller: www.neteller.com. Getting setup with NETeller or another similar company, will take some time, but with patience and a little work, you'll get it done. Hey, these companies want you to play too!

You can also wire funds into your online account, which will be on the quick side, or send a check, which will be on the very slow side, as the check would have to be received and cleared before the money would be available.

Okay, once this is achieved, there is one final step.

5. Start playing!

Get out there and have fun. And make some money!

♦ ONLINE POKER: CHECKS, BETS, CALLS, RAISES, FOLDS ♦

Get familiar with your site's betting action buttons, which will be prominently displayed on the bottom of your playing screen. When it's your turn to play, you'll make your betting decision—check, fold, call, bet, raise, or go all-in!—and execute it by clicking on the appropriate button.

♠ Time Limits

Online poker is similar to regular face-to-face poker: if you take too long to act, you will be asked to make your move or be automatically folded. The difference is that the game online has a running clock and fellow players don't have to ask a floorman to come over and "put a clock" on you.

Online poker sites give you a certain amount of time to make a decision, usually a minute. You will be alerted with a series of beeps as the clock runs down. However, if you take too long to act, the program will automatically fold your hand, regardless of the cards you hold. This feature prevents any one player from holding up the game.

If you or another player continually push the time limit to the maximum, the other players at the table will get annoyed, just as in a live game. Everyone is there to play, not watch and wait. Just like you. If you keep stalling, your opponents won't want to play with you—unless you're losing lots of money, in which case, they'll find a way to persevere.

♠ What happens if you suddenly lose your connection?

First, don't worry. All the un-bet money you had on the table is still yours; your bankroll won't be affected. If you had $1,057 in your bankroll when you got disconnected, you'll have $1,057 in it when you reconnect. Unless you win the hand that you were involved in, in which case you'd have more.

Here's how that works.

If you were involved in a pot, the program triggers an automatic stop to all betting and plays the hand as if there was an all-in, even though active players might still have more chips. The rest of the cards will be played out with the best hand at the showdown winning. Any uncalled bets will be returned to players with all called bets being part of the pot. For example, if you're on the turn, and bet $25, and an opponent loses his connection (or you lose yours), the program will return the $25 since it was not yet called. It will throw up a screen explaining the connection loss, play out the remaining cards, and award the pot to the best hand on the river.

Online sites can detect connection loss and are able to determine when this feature gets triggered. This "all-in" feature protects players who get caught in this predicament, but at the same time, there is a limit to the number of times a player can get credit for a connection loss (as there are players who will abuse this privilege by purposely ending their connection on hands they wish to see through the end without betting more).

Each online site will trigger this differently. Be sure to check out your site's disconnection policy before you play to see how that particular type of situation will get handled.

♦ ELEVEN ADVANTAGES OF ONLINE POKER ♦

If you are new to the world of playing on the Internet, here are eleven advantages that may persuade you to join the online poker craze.

1. Play Anytime

At any time of the day or night, all you have to do is go over to your computer, log on to your poker site of choice, and off you go. You're playing! There is nothing easier than that. It doesn't matter what you are wearing—or not wearing!—or how you look. You don't have to travel to a cardroom and search for the right game; with thousands of players online at any time, there is always a game with the stakes you want to play waiting for you. Keep the car in the garage. Save the gas. Just click and go.

2. Convenience

You can roll out of bed, crawl over to your computer, log in, and you're in a game. It can't get any more convenient than that. Actually, it can. Keep the computer in bed and log in when you turn over. Warning: any company you may keep in bed won't appreciate the competition.

3. Great Choice of Games

You can find any brand of hold'em on the Internet and for most any stakes. Limit, no-limit, pot-limit, small stakes, medium stakes, high stakes, penny-ante, free-play, ring games, tournaments, sit-and-goes, satellites, ring games, shorthanded, heads-up, etc.—you name it, there is a game for you.

4. No Waiting

Seats are always available. You're in the biggest poker capital of the world—the Internet. Hundreds of sites are just one click away. With more than ten thousand poker games to choose from, you'll find one with a seat open that fits the bill.

5. You Save Poker Money

There's no dealer, floormen, cocktail waitresses, or runners to tip, and the rakes are lower than in traditional poker rooms. You get more bang for your gambling buck. That leaves more money on the table for you to keep—or win.

6. They Give You Money to Play

Did I say they give you money? Yes! Online sites fiercely compete for your business, so they offer all sorts of free-money bonus deals to get you to play on their site. Read the requirements carefully, put some money in your bankroll, and show them what you got.

7. It's Good Social Fun

Poker fires up that competitive spirit and is a great social outlet as well. You may not be able to see your opponents live, but that won't stop you from being able to communicate with them. Just as in a live game, you *can* interact with your tablemates. The chat windows in online sites allow you to type messages back and forth to your fellow players.

8. Make Friends Around the World

Internet poker is now a worldwide phenomenon and it is not uncommon to see players at your table from a variety of countries. Like everything else, you eventually strike up friendships and you never know, you may soon be visiting some of your Internet poker buddies—or receiving them. Many great friendships have started online.

9. It's Great Practice for Live Games

Online poker moves much faster than regular live games so you get to see lots of hands and situations. You can practice skills that you'll be able to apply to your regular tournament or cash game.

10. Play for Money or Play for Free

You can play poker for free on pretty much every site, a service online poker rooms offer their customers so they can get acclimated to the software. Or, if you prefer, you can sign up and play for real money.

11. It's Profitable

Online players are generally much weaker than competitors you'll find in regular cash games, especially at the low limit games. This makes it very profitable for good players. If you're a really skilled player, it's more than a good way to make money, it's a great way to make a living!

♦ QUICK ONLINE STRATEGY TIPS ♦

Online players tend to play too many hands and see too many showdowns. You can profit from this by playing solid straightforward poker, extracting maximum value from your good hands and minimizing losses with your weak and marginal hands. With more players seeing the flop on average, you want to tighten up a little on the selection of hands you play.

Aggressive betting becomes even more important online, especially in no-limit. You need to limit the field to protect your premium hands. Avoid bluffing in loose games—you can't bluff players who won't fold—and give loose opponents less credit for having strong hands.

Like poker played in any form and in any setting, learning how your opponents play and adjusting your strategy accordingly will bring you the most profits.

One unique feature of online poker sites is the option players have to make a playing decision in advance, before play reaches their position, by using the **early-action buttons**. And while there are no physical tells in online poker, the frequent use of these early-action buttons can give you information about an opponents' hands. For example, if you see almost instant checks or raises when the action reaches a player, quite often, that indicates that the player has pre-selected his action. In the first case, the check probably means he is weak, and in the latter, he is either strong or he decided that he was going to bluff at the pot regardless of the action that preceded him.

The key element here is that the player decided in *advance* what his play was going to be, without even considering how the betting might go. So with garbage, a player may select the Check/Fold button, which will fold his hand if there is a bet or check if there is not.

Also look out for players who frequently use the pre-select options and then break the pattern by taking time in a situation. That could be useful information, but at the same time, it could also be indicative that the player was busy doing something else—on the phone, checking email, or in another game! But do pay attention to the timing of an opponent's reactions, and you can pick up online tells that you can use to your advantage. And pay attention to your own tendencies as well. You're not the only one watching!

Once you get comfortable online, you may find it profitable to play two games at the same time, which will allow for lots of hands and lots of possibilities. Some action junkies (and pros) looking to maximize the number of hands they receive, may play up to three or four games simultaneously! If you are considering playing multiple games, which can get confusing, remember one key tip: avoid playing tricky marginal hands that show little long-term profit! The concentration you need to finesse victories with these marginal hands will be difficult when you're flying back and forth between multiple games. Profits in the other games will suffer as your concentration is focused on the marginal hand.

If you're a tournament player, there are an endless number of choices, some of which are for straight prize money and some which award seats to the main events in the World Series of Poker and World Poker Tour tournaments as prizes for the top finishers.

♦ PLAYING ONLINE SAFELY ♦

For the most part, playing online poker is safe. Many new players are concerned with being cheated by the online software. While this is possible, and I certainly cannot guarantee or vouch for the integrity of anyone else's business practices, online poker rooms would enjoy no benefit in offering games where they manipulated the software or altered the random distribution of cards. This would be foolhardy and outright stupid on the part of the casinos. Online rooms make their money through the rake and want nothing more than the most honest game possible. And believe me, they make so much money dealing a legitimate game that there is no possible gain they could get from cheating.

This does not mean there isn't cheating. However, it's not the online poker rooms you need to be wary of—it's the players! There is collusion in certain games; sometimes by multiple players working together against unaware opponents, and sometimes an individual acts as more than one player at a table by having multiple online identities. In either case, this *is* cheating. Online poker rooms would have you believe that it never happens or that their software protects against this, but the truth is that it does occur. They do their best to prevent collusion, but they have not yet perfected the safeguards. Your best protection, as in any live face-to-face game, is to trust your instincts. If you're ever uncomfortable in a game, stop playing. Either switch tables, or if you feel uncomfortable playing on a particular site, then switch sites.

♦ FIND OUT MORE ♦

To find out more about playing on online poker sites, go to **www.cardozapub.com**.

16. MONEY MANAGEMENT

Let's begin with the most important concept for all players:

*Never gamble with money you cannot afford to
lose, either financially or emotionally.*

The short term possibilities of taking a loss are
real, no matter how easy the game may appear,
no matter how stacked the odds are in your favor.
Good players don't always win just as poor players
don't always lose. If that were not the case, losing players would
never play poker because there would be no hope of winning,
and good players would have no one to play with. There are
ups and downs in any gambling pursuit, whether you're highly
skilled, or a rank beginner.

In a poker session, any one player can beat any other player.
And that's the fun of the game. There are good days, and there
are bad days. It's just that better players will have more good
days than the bad days and will make money in the long run,
while less skilled players will have more bad days than good
days, and will end up losing money over time.

Whether you're playing cash games or tournaments, the
most important thing is to stay within your comfort zone and
play at levels you can afford. Always play at limits that won't
stress you out or put you in a vulnerable position. If rent
money is due, get off the table and pay the rent. If you've got

important bills, get them covered. You should only gamble with discretionary funds, "extra" money that you don't mind putting at risk and potentially losing.

It doesn't matter if you're the greatest player in the world. As I said above, any player can lose on any one day. And putting money that you need on the table is a bad decision.

How much should you risk? Again, it is about comfort level. Big players like Doyle Brunson, Chip Reese, or Johnny Chan can lose $250,000 in one day, but financially, it means nothing to them. It's a normal swing for the stakes they play and the risk they are accustomed to. Presumably, you don't have that kind of money to lose or the skills to even be playing that high, so this wouldn't be appropriate to you. The point is, if it hurts to lose money, even $10—emotionally, or because you need the money for bills—then you shouldn't be at the poker table in the first place.

If you're smart with your money, at worst, you'll lose your table bankroll—the exact amount you planned on risking before you hit the tables—and at best, you'll make a bundle of money and have a great time doing so. It's a simple truth: if you never play over your head, you can never get into trouble.

This is such an important concept, I'm going to repeat it:

If you never play over your head, you can never get into trouble

Find a game where you feel comfortable with the stakes, one where the betting range fits your temperament and emotional makeup. If the larger bets of a particular game make your heart pump too hard, you're over your head and need to find a game offering lower betting limits.

When you play with "scared money," you're easily bullied and pushed away from your optimum playing style. To win, you must go into the action with every asset you have, and you can't give your opponents a way to push you around because the stakes are too dear for you. Opponents will quickly figure out that you're playing scared and you'll be at a serious disadvantage.

Remember that poker is a form of entertainment and as such, must be kept in perspective. If you are preoccupied with losing money and it creates undue anxiety, the entertainment value and probably your winning expectation will slip rapidly. If that's the case, take a breather, recoup your confidence, and then hit the tables with fresh vigor. Recognizing that emotions affect the quality of play is an important step in making poker an enjoyable and profitable experience. Play only with that winning feeling.

This brings us to the very relevant question: how much should you put at risk? Let's have a look at bankrolling.

♦ BANKROLLING ♦

There are two types of bankroll requirements and both are important: table bankroll and total bankroll. **Table bankroll** is the amount of money you bring to the table and risk losing in any one session. **Total bankroll** is the amount of money you set aside to help you weather the inevitable losing streaks that occur in any form of gambling.

How do you figure out the size game you *can* play given your bankroll? Simple. First decide how much money you're willing to put at risk. If the limit you would like to play is too high for your bankroll—it's simple, you can't afford it. Find another game. Look at it this way: if you want to play at higher levels than you can currently afford, then you'll need to earn your way to the higher limit by winning at a lower level.

For example, let's say you have $300 to play with and decide to play a $10/$20 game of limit hold'em. Well, one little losing streak and you're gone. And you may not have had any bad luck, just a normal fluctuation! Let's say you drop down to $150 from the starting bankroll of $300, leaving you with $150 and a hand comes up where you like your chances. It gets three-bet preflop and flop. So you've got $30 in before the flop and $30 in on the flop for a total of $60. Well, now you're down to $90 from your pre-hand total of $150. The first player bets $20 on the turn, and while you like your chances on the hand, the problem is that you have another player behind you and another card to see. And you have only $90. Total.

You see the problem? You don't have enough money to play the game properly. And if this was a no-limit game, you'd really be playing at a disadvantage. Do you want your entire gambling bankroll devoted to one turn of the card?

So while you may like a $10/$20 game, with $300 to play with, you give yourself little chance of winning if you're undercapitalized. And undercapitalization is just as big of a handicap in poker as it is in business. If you don't have the bankroll to give yourself a fair shot to handle the inevitable rough spots, you pretty much doom your chances of succeeding from the very start.

The answer: move to a smaller game until you have enough money to play a bigger one.

♠ KEY CONCEPT ♠
Being undercapitalized in poker—or in business—virtually dooms your chances from the start.

Your bankroll requirements will vary by the game you're playing—some variations and games have bigger swings than others—however, the following guidelines will help you determine the proper amount to put at risk.

♠ Table Bankroll

As a rule of thumb, your table bankroll should be 30 times the maximum or big bet in a limit game. For example, if you're playing $10/$20, you should have $600 at your disposal to withstand the normal fluctuations of the game. This way, if you lose a few pots, you'll have enough funds remaining to continue playing with confidence. Of course, you can always run it a little looser, depending on the type of game, your playing style, and your comfort levels (maybe you'll prefer 40 times or as much as 60 times the lower bet), but this multiple of 30 is the bare minimum you should bring to the table.

Similarly, at a $1-$4 spread-limit game, you'll want $120 ($4 x 30), for a $5/$10 game, $300 ($10 x 30), and for a $30/$60 game, $1,800 ($60 x 30).

In no-limit and pot-limit games, you'll want a bigger buy-in because the fluctuation will be much greater. You generally want a big enough bankroll so that you're not at a disadvantage to your opponents. But in no case should you have less than three times the minimum buy-in for the game, with five times that amount giving you more breathing room so that you can weather the rough spots.

To figure out the limit you can afford, take your total disposable bankroll and divide it by 30. Thus, if you have $600 available and divide that by 30, you get $20. That lets you know you have enough money to play a $10/$20 game.

♠ Total Bankroll

If you casually play poker with friends once a week or in cardrooms as a recreational activity, you don't need to be so concerned about a total poker bankroll, just what you're willing to risk in that one game. You can look at it as an allowance for your Friday night or once-in-a-while game.

However, if you plan on playing poker on a serious, semi-professional, or professional level, you need to have enough money set aside to sustain the normal fluctuations common to any gambling pursuit. You'll want that total bankroll to be at least 300 times the size of the big bet to be properly financed in limit games. For example, in a $5/$10 game, you'll want a total bankroll of $3,000, and if you're playing $10/$20, you'll need $6,000.

If you're playing pot-limit or no-limit poker, you'll want more like 500 times the size of the big blind to handle the greater volatility of those betting structures.

The bankroll requirements stated in this section will give you enough breathing room to withstand losing streaks and still have enough money to come back and play pressure-free poker.

Remember, no matter how good you are as a player or how weak the level of competition, you can't always win. If you take a tough loss in one session, hey, it happens. Take a breather, catch some fresh air, and come in to the next game with new energy and the feeling of a winner. You should only play when you're feeling fresh and brimming with confidence.

♦ TOURNAMENT BANKROLL REQUIREMENTS ♦

In straight tournaments without rebuys or add-ons, you can only lose your entry fee. Not a penny more. So it is very easy to figure out your bankroll limitations for tournaments.

In tournaments with rebuys and add-ons, you want to restrict yourself to two or three extra buy-ins plus the maximum add-ons allowed if you're still in the event when the rebuy period ends. Of course, if the tournament allows unlimited rebuys, you can keep buying every time you lose your stack, but that is not the wisest policy. Put it this way: if two or three rebuys won't get it done, perhaps you should wait for another tournament or another day to try your luck again.

If you plan on entering tournaments on a regular basis, you need to figure out what you can afford. While you can only lose a certain amount in one tournament, you can lose an unlimited amount by playing an unlimited number of tournaments. If they're small entry fee tournaments, you may not give too much thought to their cost, except of course, if you're on a tight budget. You can look at these expenses the same as other types of entertainment—a ballgame, concert, or movie. But if you plan on regularly playing big events (the $1,000, or even the $10,000, entry-fee tournaments), you need to map out a budget and see if you can afford the costs. Sure, it's nice to dream of hitting it big, but don't let the dreams turn into nightmares. You must manage your money to guide you through the dry spells.

The reality of tournaments—and this is very unlike the cash games—is that long, dry spells are common when the fields are large. It is not uncommon to find many top players being shut out from cashing in *any* of the events played at the World Series of Poker championships—and there are over 40 events played. You have to look at the big picture before putting your money at risk. Set your limits before you get into action, and strictly follow the guidelines you've planned out *beforehand*.

♦ KNOW WHEN TO QUIT ♦

Part of the successful money management formula is knowing when to quit. You won't always be at the top of your game; you may be exhausted after hours of play, annoyed with another player, or simply frustrated by bad hands. Whatever the case may be, the important thing to realize is that you're distracted and that the loss of concentration will hurt your play. It's time to take a break.

You may even find yourself in a game where everything's going your way and you're winning in a big way, but getting tired. You feel you're a superior player, but you're starting to make mistakes. You hate to leave such a choice table. What to do?

Leave. Once you start making mistakes, it means you've lost your edge and you may start handing back your winnings. Of course, it's tough to leave a game you feel is ripe for your skills, but when the edge is gone, it's gone.

Take your winnings home with you.

♦ MAXIMIZING WINS AND MINIMIZING LOSSES ♦

There is a saying among professional players that goes like this: life is one-long poker game. This means that you shouldn't sweat your losses on any one session or even on a few sessions. If you're bankrolling yourself properly and playing within your means, you've got lots or room to have a good session and put some wins back into your bankroll.

Wins just won't be there every day. Once you get it through your head that you can't win every time, you'll be able to *accept* losing and get comfortable with this concept so that the times you do lose, you'll be able to restrict your losses to a reasonable amount.

To be a winner, you have to able to lose. You can't win every session just as you can't win every hand, but if you're good, you will win more than you will lose. While it's important to maximize your winnings at every session, it's equally important to minimize your losses as well.

Three quick principles follow from this:

1. Limit the Amount of Money You Can Lose at Any One Session and Plan This Out in Advance

It makes no difference how weak your perceived opponents might be or how profitable the game appears to be. Sometimes it just won't be your day. Recognize that and avoid putting yourself in a position where you lose so much in one day that you can't easily dig out of the hole.

There's always another day.

2. Never Restrict Winnings

When you're hot, you're hot. If you're winning, keep going, going, going... If you're on a roll and playing good poker or even if you feel you're incredibly lucky, hey, there's nothing wrong with that. Go for it, and keep going for it. If the money is pouring in, why stop it? However, once you've lost you're winning feeling, that's it.

3. Play Only When You Feel Like You Can Win at the Game

There are two parts to this.

a. Only play when you're confident. It's hard to win when you're not at your best or are playing scared poker.

b. Recognize when you are outclassed and move to a game where you're the king fish in a smaller bowl.

17. HOLD'EM GLOSSARY

Ace-Anything: An ace with any other card.

Act: To bet, raise, fold, or check.

Active Player: Player still in competition for the pot.

Add On: Purchase additional chips in an add-on tournament.

Add-On Tournament: A tournament that allows players a final purchase of additional chips.

Ante: Mandatory bet placed into the pot by all players before the cards are dealt.

Average Stack: In a tournament, having about equal the average number of chips held by players.

Bet: Money wagered and placed into the pot.

Big Blind: The larger of two mandatory bets made by the player two seats to the left of the dealer button position.

Big Pair: A pair of jacks, queens, kings, or aces.

Big Cards: Two non-paired cards jack or higher.

Big Slick: The A-K as starting cards.

Big Stack: In a tournament, having more than double the average amount of chips in play.

Blinded Off: In a tournament, having lost all or most of one's chips to the blinds and antes without playing a hand.

Bluff: To bet or raise with an inferior hand for the purpose of intimidating opponents into folding their cards and making the bluffer a winner by default.

Board: The face-up cards shared by all players. Also *Community Cards*.

Bubble: In a tournament, the point at which all remaining players will win money except for the next player eliminated.

Button: The player occupying the dealer position who goes last in all rounds except the preflop; also the disk used to indicate this position.

Buy-In: A player's investment of chips in a poker game or the actual amount of cash he or she uses to "buy" chips for play.

Call: To match an amount equal to a previous bet on a current round of betting.

Calling Station: An unflattering term for a player who calls too many bets and rarely raises.

Card Protector: A chip or small ornament used to indicate a hand is live and protect it from getting fouled.

Cardoza's 4 & 2 Rule: A simple formula to figure out the approximate chances of winning a hand by multiplying the number of outs on the flop by four and on the turn by two.

Cardroom Manager: Cardroom supervisor in charge of the poker games.

Cash: To win money in a tournament; currency used instead of chips to play poker or with which to buy chips.

Cash Game: Poker played for real cash money (as opposed to a tournament).

Check: The act of "not betting" and passing the bet option to the next player while still remaining an active player.

Check and Raise: A player's raising of a bet after already checking in that round.

Chop: To divide the pot equally with one or more players as a result of a tie between winning hands.

Community Cards: The face up cards shared by all players. Also *Board*.

Conservative Player: A player who tends to call rather than raise, and check rather than bet.

Correct Odds: A situation in which there is a long term expectation of breaking even or making a profit.

Cowboys: Pair of kings.

Cut Card: A special colored plastic card that is not part of the deck that is used specifically for the purpose of cutting the cards.

Cutoff Seat: The seat immediately before the button.

Dealer: The player or casino employee who shuffles the cards and deals them out to the players.

Early Position: Approximately the first third of players to act in a nine- or 10-player game or the first or second to act in a six- or seven-handed game.

Emergency Short Stack: In a tournament, having less than five times the size of the big blind bet.

Face Down: A card positioned such that its rank and suit faces the table and cannot be viewed by competing players. Cards dealt this way are also known as *Downcards*.

Face Up: A card positioned such that its rank and suit faces up and is therefore visible to all players. Cards dealt this way are also known as *Upcards* or *Open Cards*.

Fifth Street: The river; the fifth board card.

Final Table: In a tournament, the last table of players.

Flop: The first three cards simultaneously dealt face up for community use by all active players.

Flush: Hand containing five cards of the same suit.

Flush Draw: Four cards of the same suit needing one more card to form a flush.

Fold: Get rid of one's cards, thereby becoming inactive in the current hand and ineligible to play for the pot.

Four-of-a-Kind: Hand containing four cards of identical value, such as 9-9-9-9, four nines.

Free Card: A betting round where all players have checked, thereby allowing players to proceed to the next round of play without cost.

Freeze-out Tournament: A tournament in which players may not purchase additional chips—once they lose their chips, they're eliminated.

Full House: Hand consisting of three cards in one rank and two in another, such a 7-7-7-Q-Q.

Hammer: In no-limit, a big intimidating bet or raise or the threat of one.

Hand: The cards a player holds; the best five cards a player can present.

Head-to-Head: Hand or game played by two players only, one against the other. Also *Heads-Up.*

Hole Cards: Card held by a player whose value is hidden from other players.

Image: How a player's betting and playing style is perceived by his opponents—for example tight, loose, conservative, or aggressive.

Implied Odds: See **Potential Gain**.

In the Money: To win a cash prize in a tournament.

Late Position: The last two or three seats in a nine- or 10-player game, or the last or next-to-last in a game with five to seven players.

Level: A specified period of time in a tournament, marked by increased blinds or antes.

Limit Poker: Betting structure in which the minimum and maximum bet sizes are set at fixed amounts, usually in a two-tiered structure such as $5-$10.

Limp: Call a bet as a way to enter the pot cheaply.

Loose Player: A player who plays too many hands and stays in pots too long.

Main Pot: The original pot in a hand where a side pot is formed due to a player running out of chips.

Medium Pair: A pair of eights, nines, or tens (and sometimes sevens).

Medium Stack: See **Average Stack**.

Middle Position: Approximately the second third of players to act in a nine- or 10-player game or the third or fourth to act in a six- or seven-handed game.

Minimum Ideal Stack: In a tournament, having at least 25 times the size of the big blind.

Money Management: A strategy used by smart players to preserve their capital and avoid unnecessary risks.

Muck: To fold.

No-Limit: Betting structure in which the maximum bet allowed is limited only by the amount of money the bettor has on the table.

"No Set, No Bet": Advice to fold on the flop if a pair does not improve to a three of a kind hand.

Nut Flush: The best possible flush given the cards on board.

Nut Flush Draw: A draw to the best possible flush given the cards on board.

Nut Straight: The best possible straight given the cards on board.

Nut Straight Draw: A draw to the best possible straight given the cards on board.

Nuts: The best hand possible given the cards on board.

One Pair: Hand containing two cards of the same rank, such as Q-Q or 7-7.

Online Poker: Poker played on the Internet as opposed to "live" poker, in which players are actually seated together at a physical table.

Outs: Cards that will improve a hand that is behind enough to be a likely winner.

Overbet: To make a bet that is greater than one and one-half the size of the pot.

Overcard: A hole card higher in rank than any board card. For example, a jack is an overcard to a flop of 10-6-2.

Overpair: A pair higher than any card on board.

Pocket Cards: The two face-down cards received by all players.

Pocket Rockets: Two aces as starting cards.

Position: A player's relative position to the player acting last in a poker round.

Pot: The sum total of all antes, blinds, and bets placed in the center of the table by players during a poker hand.

Potential Gain: The amount of chips that can potentially be won (assuming opponents will make additional bets) compared to the cost of a bet. Also **Implied Odds**.

Pot-Limit: Betting structure in which the largest bet can be no more than the current size of the pot.

Pot Odds: The amount of money in the pot compared to the cost of a bet. For example if $50 is in the pot, and a player needs to call a bet of $10 to play, he is getting pot odds of 5 to 1.

Pot-Sized Bet: A bet that is about the size of the pot.

Power Play: A hand that is believed to be inferior, but is played strongly by betting or raising in an attempt to drive opponents out of a pot.

Preflop: The first betting round in hold'em, when each player has only their two pocket cards.

Premium Starting Hands: One in a group of the best starting cards in hold'em: A-A, K-K, Q-Q, and A-K, and sometimes A-Q and J-J as well.

Prize Pool: The total amount of money in a tournament that will be awarded to the winners.

Raise: A wager that increases a previous bet.

Rake: The amount of money taking out of the pot by the house as its fee for running the game.

Rebuy: To purchase additional chips.

Rebuy Tournament: A tournament that allows players to purchase additional chips during the specified period of time, usually the first few rounds of play.

Reraise: To raise another player's raise.

Resteal: On the first betting round, to bluff a raiser who is attempting to steal the blinds out of a pot.

Ring Game: A cash game with a full table of players, usually seven or more.

River: The fifth community card on board.

Round: See **Level**.

Royal Flush: An A-K-Q-J-10 of the same suit. The highest ranking hand in hold'em.

Satellite: One or two table mini-tournament.

Set: Three of a kind.

Shorthanded: A poker game played with seven players or less.

Short Stack: In a tournament, having less than ten times the big blind.

Showdown: The final act in a poker game, where remaining players reveal their hands to determine the winner of the pot.

Side Pot: A separate pot created for players who are still betting on a hand in which an active bettor has run out of chips.

Short-Handed: Poker played with less than the normal number of players, usually seven or fewer.

Short Stack: In a tournament, having less than ten times the size of the big blind bet.

Slowplay: To bet a strong hand weakly to disguise its strength and trap an opponent.

Small Blind: The smaller of two mandatory bets made by the player sitting immediately to the left of the dealer button position.

Small Pair: A pair of sevens or less.

Speculative Play: A hand believed to be a longshot to win, but because of its speculative nature, would hold surprise strength if the hand improves.

Standard Raise: A preflop raise of three times the big blind.

Steal the Blinds: On the first betting round, bluff opponents out of a pot no one has entered so that the blinds can be won.

Straight: A sequence of five consecutive cards of mixed suits, such as 4-5-6-7-8.

Straight Draw: Four cards in sequence needing one more card to form a straight.

Straight Flush: A sequence of five consecutive cards in the same suit, such as 8-9-10-J-Q all of spades.

String Bet: Additional chips added to a bet that has already been placed, which is disallowed.

Suited Connectors: Consecutive cards that are of the same suit, such as 9-10 of hearts.

Super Satellite: A low buy-in multiple table tournament that awards the top finishers with entry into a bigger buy-in event.

Table Bankroll: The amount of money a player has on the table or has set aside for play.

Table Stakes: A rule stating that a player's bet or call of a bet is limited to the amount of money he has on the table in front of him.

Tapped-Out: A player who has no more funds from which to bet—he's broke.

Tells: Body language, expressions, or mannerisms that reveal information about the strength of a player's hand.

Three of a Kind: Poker hand containing three cards of the same rank, such as 4-4-4.

Tight Player: A player who plays only premium hands and enters few pots.

Tight-Aggressive: A style of player in which a player enters few pots but when he does, he bets and raises aggressively.

Total Bankroll: The total amount of money a player has set aside as his gambling stake.

Tournament: A competition in which players start with an equal number of chips and play until one player holds all them.

Tournament Chips: Chips used specifically for tournaments and that have no cash value.

Tournament Director: The supervisor responsible for organizing and running a tournament.

Trap: To induce a player to put more chips into a pot in which he is almost a sure loser.

Trips: Three of a kind.

Trouble Hands: Starting cards, such as A-J and K-Q, which can lose lots of chips by connecting with the flop by being outkicked or outpaired by bigger cards held by an opponent.

Turn: The fourth community card on board.

Two Pair: Poker hand containing two sets of two cards of the same rank, such as J-J-5-5.

Underbet: To make a bet that is one-third smaller than the size of the pot or less.

Under the Gun: The first player to act in a round of poker.

Washing: To randomly mix the cards on the table.

WPT: World Poker Tour.

WSOP: World Series of Poker.